MW00905563

Augustina

AUGUSTINA

A Novel based on a True Story

written by Melanie Dawn Larinde

ISBN 9781723723810

Dedication

This book is dedicated to my mother, in love and gratitude, who wished to tell the story of her mother, Augustina.

Acknowledgements

I first want to acknowledge my husband, Mark, for giving me the freedom and flexibility to work on this book, and providing me a wonderful workspace in which to do so. I want to thank my children, Coby and Nicole, for being independent and self-sufficient, unknowingly affording me the time to write this book. I want to thank Annie and Jean Chabannier, for graciously offering me a room in their beautiful home in the South of France where a majority of the finishing touches were made on this book. And I want to thank my special longtime friend and *copine*, Dawn Forman, who is the quickest person I know to respond to my texts - morning or evening - who reviewed this book, and who always stood by my side.

Table of Contents

Chapter One

Augustina hurried along Spring Street in downtown Los Angeles on that early June morning in 1965, wearing a gray plaid mid-calf length skirt that she had cut and sewn from a homemade pattern, accompanied by a cream colored blouse and gray jacket, rounding out the ensemble with a red silk scarf fastidiously tied around her neck. It was rare that Augustina went out, especially to downtown, so extra care was given to ensure her outfit suited its particular purpose.

Although as long as she could remember in her 75 years, Augustina had admired nature and everything it had to offer in the way of seasonal foliage, annuals and perennials for outdoor flower beds, and the shiny green leaves on her indoor philodendron, today she did not look up once to notice the blossoming trees planted every 100 or so feet along the urban parkway. Her eyes were fixed on the numbers mounted atop the skyscrapers' immense plate glass double door entrances.

Slung from her left shoulder was a large, worn, brown leather bag which she clutched tightly in her left hand, pressed against her side. In her right hand she carried a paper with a handwritten name and address on it, which she repeatedly referred to as she checked the numbers on the skyscrapers.

When she arrived at the building whose numbers matched those written on the paper in her hand, both purpose and trepidation ran through her veins as she walked up the expansive steps and entered the 20-story formal black building.

⁂

Chapter Two

The sun was setting over the small town of Sedovna, Poland on this Fall day of 1897. Peace prevailed throughout the flourishing farmland of the quiet countryside, a stunning contrast to the noisy, over-crowded cities of the western world today.

"Come on, Augustina!" cried Paulina.

Responding to her sister's call, seven-year-old Augustina – a rosy-cheeked, black-eyed peasant girl with long chestnut brown wavy hair that flew in the wind in all directions - ran across a field toward the horse-drawn wagon loaded with fresh picked crops. Her worried looking father, Heinrich, was sitting beside her 9-year-old brother, Gottlieb. The father was a handsome man in rugged farm clothes with rough hands and a battered straw hat. Two dogs sat in the rear of the wagon, barking and wagging their tails happily as little Augustina approached.

Her German family had settled in Poland after the war. Many Poles hated the Germans who historically were their conquerors. Augustina's intensity and skepticism were already apparent. At the early age of seven, she had learned to fight back, defending herself and her siblings against slurs of Polish children who more and more frequently adopted the taunts and prejudices of their outspoken parents toward all Germans.

Augustina caught up with the wagon as her concerned father exclaimed, "Hurry! We have to get home to your mother!" Brother Gottlieb grabbed her hand and hoisted her up onto the seat beside him.

With one handed intention, Heinrich flicked the horse's rump, as they all headed back to the farmhouse where Augustina's older sisters would have supper waiting on the table.

As the wagon approached the house, three dashing Cossacks in splendid uniform, swords gleaming at their sides, came galloping up behind them on spirited horses. Brother Gottlieb sucked in his astonished breath and pointed at them, crying with excitement, "Look!"

Augustina's eyes popped open wide when she saw the Cossacks astride their snorting steeds charge to a halt in front of their house, flamboyant Oleg leading the way. Heinrich's sister had married a Russian when she was very young, and now the husband was a Cossack, a member of a militaristic community based in southern Russia. With a huge grin on his face, Heinrich pulled the wagon to a stop, not far from the front door.

Augustina jumped down from the wagon and ran to the house shouting, "Paulina! Amelia!" Gottlieb and his father got down off the wagon and approached the Cossacks. Alerted by Augustina's cry, her four-year-old sister Maria stumbled around the side of the house with berry juice running down the front bodice of her dress, carrying a basket half-filled with wild berries she had been picking. Paulina and Amelia ran out of the house and stared at the impressively uniformed Cossacks and their prancing horses. Three of their neighbors hurried over to join them - Stanislas and two plump women.

Augustina knew nothing of the terror of the Cossacks or the Russians who governed her country, or, for that matter, much about anything outside her simple life on the farm. To have a magnificently-uniformed Cossack for an uncle was a breath-taking event for her!

Oleg came down off his horse and exchanged boisterous greetings with his brother-in-law Heinrich. In a loud, exuberant voice, Oleg introduced his two Cossack companions, as their horses' restless feet danced about, anxious to go on. Heinrich introduced the neighbors: Stanislas, a large, rough-looking farmer with a limp - that morning Stanislas had a painful accident while pushing his hand plow in the field, which was why he was home; and two neighboring wives, Tamara and Stephania.

Then, turning his attention to his left, amazed, Oleg stared at the children and said, "Surely *these* cannot be your children! Heinrich, they are all so big!" He remembered five little children the last time he was there. Heinrich proudly said, "Yes, they're growing up!" Oleg greeted each one in turn and proved to them that he remembered their names: Paulina, the oldest and the tallest, age 13; Amelia, age 12; Gottlieb, the brother, age 9; Augustina, age 7; and Maria, the baby, age 4.

Looking around, the Cossack wanted to know, "And where is their mother?"

Heinrich wrinkled his brow and sighed. "Gisela," he said, "is very ill. A few days ago she came down with violent stomach pains, and she's still in bed. The doctor doesn't know what it is, but thinks it's food poisoning. Stanislas's wife, Irena, is taking care of her."

The front door of the house burst open. Grief-stricken sobs filled the air. Heinrich and the others whirled around as Irena rushed toward them crying out in anguish that Gisela was dead. Screaming and weeping, the children ran into the house. Heinrich gasped and trembled as they stumbled inside together. Oleg clapped an arm around his brother-in-law's shoulders to support him. The other two Cossacks waited outside.

Gisela lay on the bed under a handmade patchwork quilt. The children's sobs filled the room. Grief-stricken, Heinrich fell down on his knees beside the bed and wept loudly. Dumbfounded with shock, the neighbors followed them into the house.

Choking on her tears, Augustina threw herself on the bed beside her mother's body. Heinrich stood up and lifted her roughly away from the bed, but she struggled until she released his grasp, then flung herself back on her mother's body. He could not comfort her.

The other two Cossacks stepped inside the doorway, solemnly joining the grieving faces. On that somber afternoon in September, it was as if the entire world had come crashing down for each member of Augustina's family.

Gisela's funeral took place a few days later in a local church with a fair amount of attendees. Though a quiet woman whose primary task was staying home taking care of her five children while her husband worked on the farm and travelled when necessary to keep the family business afloat, her kind smile and thoughtful words whenever she greeted a neighbor on the street gained her the reputation of a well-liked woman, and it was virtually impossible for anyone in her town to speak a negative word about her.

Barely three months later, on a dreary winter's day, still saddened by her mother's death, Augustina was lugging a wooden bucket of water from the well toward the house. She tripped on a rock and fell on her right knee, dropping the bucket, spilling the water. Rubbing her smarting knee, she sat down near a bank of tall shrubs. She was about to cry out loud when she heard distraught voices on the other side of the bushes, coming from people hidden from her view. Peeking around the bushes, she saw her neighbors, Stanislas, still limping a little, and Irena and Tamara walking toward her up the dirt road, unaware of her presence. They looked as if a bombshell had just been thrown into their midst. As their emotions rose, they stopped walking only feet from her. Augustina could hear their every word. Her father Heinrich, they said, had married another woman in Warsaw and was bringing her home!

They were shocked at how quickly after the death of her dear mother Gisela that Heinrich had remarried! It was a disgrace!

That poor, sweet woman had *lived* for that man, and he'd forgotten her already! None of his neighbors were invited to the wedding. His *children* didn't even *know* about it! "He never mentioned her to anybody, and if I hadn't seen the two of them with my own eyes last week when I went into town, I would never have known of her existence. It's a crying shame!" declared Tamara.

Hidden on the other side of the shrubbery, Augustina gasped. She cupped both hands hard over her mouth to keep from crying out.

Stanislas reminded Irena and Tamara that Heinrich's neighbors and former friends had been making numerous accusations ever since Gisela's death and that was no doubt the reason Heinrich didn't *dare* invite them to his wedding.

A week or so back, the day before his departure on his journey to Warsaw, Heinrich confided in Stanislas behind the barn that he would be bringing his new wife home in a few days. A delivery boy, overheard and unbeknownst to the men, took this news back to town. The word was out that the new woman had no parents to pay for the wedding. It was a barren ceremony with just the two of them standing before a magistrate.

"How could they do it so soon after the mother died!" moaned Irena.

"It's the children we have to pity," said Tamara bitterly. "To have such a beast for a father! Poor little ones."

"But what could Heinrich do?" asked Stanislas, spreading his arms wide in question. "Five children! He has to have somebody take care of them and the house and help with the farm, doesn't he? He was lucky to find a *new* wife so soon!"

Tamara and Irena whirled on him. "To *find* her?" Tamara spat back at him. "He obviously *had* her a long time! I wasn't the only one who saw them together. Everybody knew how he used to meet her in Warsaw even before poor Gisela died! He poisoned

Gisela! He did it for her farm and the money he inherited from her so he could marry this—this tramp!"

Stanislas admonished her not to talk like that!

"It's true. I tell you," yelled Tamara. Heinrich brought nothing to the marriage. The farm was Gisela's from her father. Now it will be Heinrich's and that other woman's!"

"And he'll be in charge of the children's share till they're old enough to take possession," said Irena. "Seriously, what can you really expect from a German?"

"But the doctor said there's no proof it was anything else besides food poisoning," said the man.

"And who poisoned the food?" interrupted Tamara pointedly.

"Nobody had to poison it," insisted the man. "It could have been spoiled food and they didn't know it."

"Aw, go on! Nobody else died, did they?" said Irena. "Don't make excuses for him, Stanislas. He already had his next woman picked out."

As they walked on, their voices faded away from horrified Augustina, who by this time had a stream of tears violently but silently rolling down her cheeks. Although she was only seven years old, and did not understand the full impact of her father's actions, she certainly understood deep down that something was significantly wrong with what her father did, with what happened to her mother, and what all the neighbors were secretly saying about her entire family.

A few days later, the sound of horses' hooves and the rumble of buggy wheels on the dirt road were heard approaching Heinrich's farmhouse, where Stanislas's wagon was parked outside. Inside the house, the excited neighbors and children hurried to the window and peered out.

"It's them!" cried Irena.

The five children crowded in close behind her, vying for space to see their father and the despised woman he was bringing with him into the only home they had ever known. Augustina, tears filling her eyes, pushed her way to the front.

The horse and buggy pulled up before the house and stopped behind Stanislas's wagon. Heinrich, all dressed up in city clothes, was holding the reins, nervously reacting to the sight of Stanislas's wagon parked out front. An attractive, anxious woman of twenty-nine, sat rigidly on the seat beside him, laughing appreciatively at something Heinrich said that could not be heard by those on the other side of the window, hard as they tried to decipher the words spoken between the newly married couple.

Inside, the two neighbor women whispered to each other that it was unbelievable how Heinrich was bringing *That Woman* here, still unable to forgive him for not inviting them to the wedding.

"Her name is Frieda," said Stanislas confidently.

Seeing the ring on Frieda's finger, the two women immediately noticed it was quite a bit bigger than Gisela's wedding ring.

From inside the house, the children watched their smiling father help Frieda step from the buggy, then pull two bulky suitcases down and start toward the house. His bride followed a few steps behind him. She seemed breathless and jittery, but otherwise happy. Heinrich steadied himself in anticipation of what he knew awaited them inside, then with cautious intent opened the front door.

As they entered the house, the newlyweds were confronted by the accusing stares of the neighbors hovering protectively around the children. Heinrich and Frieda stopped laughing. The new bride's face turned white. Heinrich's face turned red with anger.

"This is my new wife, Frieda," he told the crowd callously. There were several moments of cold silence, then Stanislas stepped up and shook hands with the trembling bride. After introducing himself, he introduced his wife, Irena, who nodded curtly. The rest of the room remained silent. The children stood staring at not only this perfect stranger, but at what they considered a blatant intruder in their own living room.

Heinrich tersely called out the names of his children and the neighbors who were present. Seeing how shaken his new wife was, he announced to the others that it was a tiring ride from Warsaw and Frieda had to get some rest. It would be better if the neighbors left – - *now*.

The neighbors gasped and looked at one another, then began shuffling out of the room.

When only the immediate family remained, Frieda took a deep sigh of relief. She looked at the baby of the family, Maria, and her face broke out in a warm smile. "What a pretty little girl!" she said, stepping forward to embrace her. Augustina quickly pulled her little sister back.

"Don't touch her!" she cried.

Livid at such behavior, Heinrich shouted at Augustina and warned all of them that *Frieda was their mother now!* Following a long period of silence, the children put on sullen faces, but remained quiet.

"Now go on out and play!" he ordered roughly.

Augustina defiantly threw an arm around Maria. As she and the other children filed out, she looked back suspiciously at Frieda.

Before departing, the visiting neighbors had huddled in the front yard, exchanging impressions of Heinrich's "guilty behavior," and the "unwelcome witch!" The children listened to their comments.

"Do you really think they did it?"

"Of course they did it!"

"That little hussy will never take the place of Gisela! Never!"

"It's not right for her and Heinrich to look so happy after they killed Gisela!"

"Do you think she was in on the plot?"

"Sure, she was! She's a German, you know! What do you expect?"

Responding to the neighbor's harsh words, in a protective tone towards her siblings, Amelia said, "God will punish them! You'll see."

As the visitors left for their respective homes, Gottlieb, Augustina and the other children looked at one another.

"Are we German?" asked little Maria.

Paulina, the oldest, snapped, "Yes!"

"Is it bad to be German?" asked Augustina.

"Some people think it is!" said Paulina.

Augustina concluded silently that if their neighbors thought it was bad to be German, then they must not really be their friends.

With the stepmother's arrival at the farm, a ten-year battle began with Frieda and Heinrich on one side, and the five children on the other.

In keeping with her own strict German upbringing, Frieda tried to control her stepchildren with shouts and orders. This stirred up a rebellion she could not control. Frieda was outnumbered and no match for the lively, hostile youngsters. The neighbors encouraged them to defy their stepmother. Even though Augustina was unsure of her neighbors' friendships now, she was even more unsure of Frieda.

One of the tasks Frieda was faced with was trying to put a stop to the children's constant raids on the larder, their large cupboard for storing food, especially when it was close to mealtime.

One day she caught little Maria sneaking a biscuit from the kitchen.

"You can't have that until after supper!" she cried. She grabbed the child and started to spank her.

Augustina, Paulina and Amelia heard Maria's screams and ran to investigate. With Augustina at the fore, they rescued their baby sister and escaped with her and the biscuit, leaving the stepmother helpless and distraught.

When Heinrich came home, Frieda was in tears. She complained of a splitting headache. She cried that she did not know if she could stand such wickedness from the children.

"They're always after the food!" she wept. "There is no discipline! They won't listen to me. Augustina will not let me teach Maria right from wrong!"

Heinrich angrily stalked outside and found Augustina with Maria and ordered them to go to bed.

"But it's still light outside!" protested Augustina.

"You will have no supper!" he said. "Maybe it will teach you to stop running in and out of the house stealing food. From now on, the food will be locked up!"

Paulina and Amelia who were helping to prepare the supper were as stunned as Augustina. Maria began to wail in protest, but there was no changing their father's mind.

Augustina and the other children considered this incident a cruel, uncalled-for punishment; a terrible betrayal by their father who had turned against them in favor of the witch he brought home with him right after their mother had died.

The years passed with constant emotional fights and upheavals becoming a regular part of the household. Encouraged by the neighbors, the children continued to defy Frieda. Augustina was always defending mischievous little Maria.

"They never give me a chance!" cried Frieda to Heinrich.

She began to fight back with fainting and crying spells, and much of the household work she would have done otherwise, now fell on the children's shoulders.

"I'm tired of Frieda pretending to have fainting spells and headaches so we have to do all her work!" complained Augustina. But Heinrich always listened to Frieda and took her side. When he was around, the children obeyed out of fear. They had not forgotten the neighbors' whispering that he was responsible for their mother's death and they were afraid to think of what he might do to them if he got angry enough.

When Augustina was fifteen years old, she had reached her full height of five-feet-one, the average height of the girls in her family. With her flashing black eyes, dark hair, and rosy cheeks, Augustina was an attractive young lady.

Augustina was hoeing in the field one cold day, bundled up in her babushka alongside Amelia, twenty, Gottlieb, seventeen, and Maria, twelve. Paulina, twenty-one, who had grown quite tall, had married a young farmer and moved away. She already had a child of her own.

Augustina stopped her work and looked toward the sun to determine the time of day. She left the field to return to the house and help Frieda with the supper, one of the tasks she was charged with.

Walking along the dirt road to the house, Augustina heard a girl's voice call out "Augustina!" She turned and saw her friend and neighbor, 11-year-old Helena, hurrying to catch up with her. Helena was on her way home from school, carrying a tablet and pencil.

When the girl reached her, Augustina asked, "Is that your school tablet?" Helena nodded.

"What's in it?" Augustina wanted to know.

Helena opened it and held it up for her to see one of the pages. Augustina, who could not read, looked curiously at the page. "What does it say?" she wanted to know.

"I forgot you can't read. It's Arithmetic" said Helena. "I have to study tonight because we're having an examination tomorrow."

As she so often did, Augustina wistfully confessed that she wished she could go to school. She had begged her father ever since she was six years old, but he always said, “Girls don’t need schooling to take care of the house and children and work in the fields.”

“I *wish* you could go!” said Helena. “We could walk to school together.”

She bade Augustina goodbye and left her at a crossroad that led to her own house. As Augustina continued on alone, a furry little rabbit darted across a field and disappeared into the brush. She came to a river, and dropped down on the bank, pulling in a deep breath of pure, clean air, dreaming that someday she, too, would go to school. A frog leaped into the water, startling her. She often paused here, watching the dragonflies flit about, and minnows swim under the clear water near the surface, marveling at how different the creatures of the earth were from people, and even from each other. It was so good to be alone for a little while in the peaceful, open country, away from the unsettling suspicions and underlying resentment that constantly plagued her home.

It was late afternoon when Augustina arrived home and walked into the kitchen.

“Did you get lost?” snapped Frieda sarcastically.

Heinrich appeared from another room, his face red with anger. “Where have you been?” he demanded. “We’ve all been waiting for you to come home, and now Supper is late!”

Augustina protested that she only took a minute to rest by the river. She worked hard in the field all day. “If you don’t believe me, go and see all the hoeing I did!” she challenged him.

Questioned sternly, she admitted that she also took a few minutes to talk to Helena who was on her way home from school. “Why can’t *I* go to school?” she cried. She sobbed that she was always treated like an animal, fed and forced to work hard, then when grown-ups talked about anything except disciplining the children, she was shooed away!

"I know I'll get a whipping for begging you again, but I want to go to school! I wanted to go to school all my life. You let Gottlieb go because he's a boy, and you let Paulina and Amelia go for two years, but not me. I want to go! I can still work in the field if you give me the pennies it takes to buy a pencil and a tablet."

To her amazement, Frieda turned to Heinrich and asked why Augustina couldn't go to school for a little while. Augustina stared at her with open mouth and Heinrich looked at his wife with piercing, impatient eyes. Finally, tired of all the arguing, he took a deep breath and turned to Augustina sternly, mumbling, "All right, you can go *this* winter. But just this one winter!"

Augustina was ecstatic.

"But it will be a waste of money!" her father shouted. He warned her she would be allowed to go only as long as she did all her chores *and gave Frieda no trouble!* "If there are any more fights between you two, NO MORE school!"

Augustina looked uncertainly at her stepmother who nodded and gave her a timid smile. Then Augustina excitedly began making her plans. "I can walk to school with Helena!" she cried.

Heinrich waved his hand in disgust. "It's a long walk for nothing!" he said. "Frieda never had any schooling and *she* doesn't miss it." Frieda said nothing but Augustina saw a fleeting desperate look in her eyes. Surprised that the witch had paved the way for her to go to school, Augustina wasn't going to argue about it!

Forgetting all about helping to prepare the supper, Augustina started to rush out and see if Gottlieb and her sisters were on their way home from the field so she could tell them the unbelievable news.

"Augustina!" yelled her father gruffly. He pointed to a large, empty pan and a pile of potatoes waiting to be peeled. She hesitated for a moment, then ran back and eagerly set about her task.

It was bitter cold and still dark that winter's morning when Augustina scurried out of bed before anyone else was stirring in the house. Drawing back the front window curtain, she looked out and saw snow falling.

She placed wood in the kitchen stove and started a fire to heat some water in a pan, then briskly scrubbed her face, neck and arms with soap. Once dressed in a clean but faded wool dress with plenty of undergarments, her sweater and heavy coat to wear over it, her knit cap and heavy gloves, she brought her pencil and tablet into the kitchen and set them down triumphantly on the table. Donning a large apron to protect her dress, she took a hunk of black bread from a tin box on the cabinet counter. She was spreading butter on it when Heinrich appeared from outside holding a pail of fresh milk from the cow. He gruffly indicated she was to drink some for her breakfast, and went out. Augustina happily breakfasted alone with black bread and warm milk.

Bundled up in her heavy clothes and gloves, clutching her pencil and tablet, Augustina braved the strong wind that whipped up as she trudged through the snow to Helena's house so they could walk to school together. In her excitement, she arrived very early.

Helena's loving peasant mother, Irena, bustled about, preparing her child for school. Augustina sat down and watched Helena finish a bowl of hearty, hot porridge, saying not a word about how she had to get ready by herself as best she could. Yet she admitted to herself how grateful she was that Heinrich brought her the fresh milk from their cow. She and her father had few things to say to one another these days. It seemed to her that he was always barking out orders to her and defending Frieda, and she, alone, was always defending herself.

The happy mother bundled Helena up, following the girls to the door and seeing them off, burying their heads against the cold, blustery wind. Augustina's head towered above that of her eleven-year-old friend.

Augustina was extremely excited and somewhat nervous as they approached the little, one-room schoolhouse. She wondered if she would be able to keep up with the small children in the first grade where she would have to sit. As she walked into the building, the children who were there ahead of them, tall and small, were scattered about the room in their seats from grades one to eight. They stared at her curiously. Augustina recognized a few of them and gave them quick smiles but did not speak. They looked surprised, as though none of them had ever expected to see her in school. One of the older girls whispered disdainfully to her neighbor about Augustina's poor clothing, but one 8th grade boy gave her an admiring glance, for she was flushed and pretty as she sat there in the front row.

Helena took her up to the teacher seated at her desk at the front of the classroom. "This is my friend Augustina," she said. "She'll be starting school today." Helena gave Augustina an encouraging smile, then went to her own seat three rows away.

The teacher bid Augustina welcome and asked what grade she was in. Augustina dropped her voice, hoping the small children in the first row would not hear her, "I've never been to school before," she said.

The teacher nodded with understanding, pointing to a seat in the front row among the smallest children. Augustina turned around and saw Helena sitting in the back with the advanced students. Being one of the biggest in the room, and thinking of the hurtful comment earlier by the rude girl about her poor clothing, Augustina felt her face flush. However, deep down, a well of triumph was building up inside, because she was finally at school...

For Augustina's benefit, the teacher announced that the lessons would be given in Russian, German, then Polish.

Augustina was glad her family spoke German and Polish at home, and she even knew a little Russian.

A month after she began school, Augustina got an eye infection which resulted in a problem seeing out of her left eye, but she never missed a day of school. Fortunate to be in the first row, she was still able to follow her lessons. The boy who liked her from the moment he saw her on her first day, was the first to be at her side and offered to help her whenever he could, making school a much more pleasant experience. Being an eighth grader, he would be graduating at the end of the term.

At home, her problems with Frieda resurfaced. Augustina had quieted down for a while after her stepmother had encouraged Heinrich to let her go to school, but she and the other children still believed that Frieda was in on the plot to kill their mother. It was not long before the old tensions were re-introduced into the family's daily routine. In fact, the situation worsened because Frieda resented Augustina's attitude and decided she had made a mistake speaking up for her. When Augustina was in school, it meant more work for Frieda at home.

In the bitter cold of that winter, Augustina walked to and from school so bundled up it was hard for her to take a normal sized step, and when she did, it was a challenge raising her foot so high up out of the snow to take the next one. This arduous routine often slowed her down. Augustina and Helena passed adult peasants on the road wearing their great, heavy clothing, with fur caps and ear muffs, thick wool socks and boots, and leggings over the boots to keep from freezing their feet. Wagons rumbled along on the roads where Augustina and Helena walked, with bundled-up drivers, who at times, when their workload permitted the extra minutes it would take, were kind enough to stop and give them a ride.

There were days and nights when no one dared open the door to the house without being bundled up the same way, for fear their feet or noses would be frozen off.

"Hurry, shut the door!" someone would cry. "You know what happened to the neighbor? His toes froze and fell off when he took off his socks."

Many times their horses, cows and pigs had to be brought into the house overnight to keep them from freezing to death in the barn.

Vegetables grown on the farm and kept for their personal consumption had to be buried in the ground in the summer and fall months to keep them fresh and cool. Throughout the winter, Heinrich dug up the ones they would wash, cut up, and cook for each meal.

Winter came and went, and the snow finally melted. Now, the blossoms of spring were once again bountiful, but the climate between Frieda and the children was far from pleasant. Toward the end of the school term when summer was approaching, Augustina had another screaming, physical clash with Frieda, over the stepmother's attempt to discipline mischievous little Maria. Augustina was so angry that she and Maria pushed Freida, knocking her down. Stunned Freida sat on the floor, unable to believe what had happened. Augustina, too, was speechless. She turned and ran from the room.

That night when Heinrich came in from the fields, he was livid to learn about the fight. He listened to Frieda's side but would not listen to Augustina's. Angrily he informed her that her school days were over. She could not go back. "It was all a bunch of foolishness anyway!" he declared.

Augustina tearfully begged to be allowed to finish out the term. It was only a few more days until the last day of school and she wanted to be there when the eighth-graders graduated. She did not tell him how much she wanted to be there to see the ceremonious moment when her boyfriend received his diploma.

Heinrich grudgingly gave his permission. Maria, who was now twelve, ran to Augustina and hugged her around the waist. Frieda started to say something to her, then turned and stomped out of the room.

The last day of school was warm and sunny. The other children wore a colorful array of pastel dresses and shirts to graduate in and celebrate the final day of school. She looked forward eagerly to seeing her special friend graduate, but she felt awful in the old, solid dark-green dress she had to wear. Quietly she told him and her friend Helena that she would not be back in the fall. Helena was as disappointed as Augustina.

The joy of attending school had ended. Her disappointments seemed too hard to bear. The boy and Helena tried to comfort her, but, though their gestures were kind, Augustina struggled to keep her otherwise usual demeanor of persistence/strong will from waning.

When it was time to go home, Augustina's boyfriend left with his parents by wagon, and Augustina started walking homeward with Helena and her mother. In tears, she sobbed that she didn't want to live in her father's house anymore. Paulina, her older sister, had asked if she would like to come and live with her and her husband and help with the care for her babies and the housework. Augustina decided to do it.

At Helena's house, her parents, Irena and Stanislas, were talking about America. The mother greeted Helena and Augustina cheerfully, then sobered and said she was so sorry this was Augustina's last day. After consoling her as best she could, the adults continued their conversation while the girls listened. Stanislas had heard that a local family was planning to escape from Poland with a small group who would travel to first to Germany and Belgium, and from there sail on a ship to America - the Land of the Free - where everybody was rich and happy.

"But what if they're caught?" worried Irena.

"They won't be," said Stanislas. "It's all arranged. It's a secret. I can't tell you anymore." They would bribe the border guard on duty. He would turn his back, and they would drive on through to the German border. The guard was acquiring quite a bit of extra cash carrying out this covert scheme.

Irena declared such a plan was too dangerous. If they were caught, they would be shot. "It's their decision" Stanislas said. He left to go back to the field to continue his work.

Augustina told Helena's mother she would like to go to a place like America someday.

"Lots of people would like to go," said Irena, "but it's too dangerous to take that chance."

Augustina defiantly said she thought she would like to do it anyway. She had always been more courageous than the rest of her family, even her older sisters, and for that matter, more courageous than almost everyone she knew. She wasn't quite sure where this sense of bravery came from. Her mother was on the quiet side, and besides Maria, her sisters were pretty obedient and predictable. But adventure was definitely part of Augustina's soul, and she knew even years before that her life ahead would be filled with new worlds, new people, and new ideas that she could only imagine in her dreams from her modest family farm in Poland.

"Even if you could go, it would take a long time for you to save enough money for such a trip," Irena said. "And even if you got the money, the risk of getting caught would be too great to take a chance on. Your home is here, Augustina. When you come of age to inherit your share of your mother's land, you will be a landowner." Helena's mother smiled. "Maybe by that time, you will meet a nice man who wants to marry you!" Confused now, Augustina thought of the boy she liked at school.

Shortly thereafter, Augustina broke free from the reigns of her father and stepmother and went to live with Paulina's family, helping with her two children, washing and changing diapers, scrubbing floors, constantly doing never-ending housework, dreaming of the day she could get away from it all and go to America.

Chapter Three

It was the Spring following Augustina's 16th birthday that previous November, and a day of torn emotions. As soon as she was legally old enough to do so, she lost no time selling the portion of the farm left to her by her mother and began detailing her plans.

Her brother and sisters were gathered around Augustina outside the farmhouse, sad, fearful, excited, in awe of the risky adventure on which she was embarking. With butterflies in her stomach and sadness gripping her throat, the big day had arrived after what seemed like an eternity of anticipation. She looked at her loving and supportive siblings – tears of joy and sorrow welling up in their eyes - and wondered if she had made the right decision. Amelia helped her pin her money, divided and wrapped tightly in two handkerchiefs, to her underclothes with large safety pins. Her few belongings were packed in two cardboard boxes, secured by ropes that also served as handles, ready for her to begin her escape from Poland on her way to America.

Gathered around her were her siblings:

Paulina, 23, married with two children;

Amelia, the most religious, age 22 and soon to be wed;

Gottlieb, age 18;

Maria, 14, weeping with the realization that her closest friend and protector, Augustina, whom she loved dearly, would no longer be there to share her life.

Augustina hugged Maria and the two sisters wept. There was not enough money for both of them to go, but she promised to write a letter as soon as she could. Thank God her father had let her go to school that one winter, and she could at least scratch a line or two to tell her family how she was doing. Gottlieb and her older sisters could read her letter and tell Maria what it said. Someday she might be able to send for Maria to come and live with her. Oh how she wished she could take her with her now!

Maria promised that when she got her own money she would come join her sister in the promised land!

Paulina worried about Augustina going alone, carrying all that money tied in her handkerchiefs, one rolled and pinned in the top of her stocking, the other pinned inside the bosom of her undershirt. This included money to escape over the border to Germany, money to take the train from Germany to Belgium, passage money for the ship to America, and money to have when she arrived, for immigrants were required to either have enough money to live off of when they landed in America, or proof that a responsible party, such as a relative or close family friend, would be there to receive them.

In the dark of night, a covered hay wagon would smuggle the little group from Poland across the border of Germany. A German guard who would be on patrol had been bribed to let them pass. It sounded so dangerous, but the two drivers who organized the daring escape had done it several times before. The bribed guard would arrive early, before the second night guard came on duty. As soon as the day guards left their post and were out of sight, the wagon would be hurried safely across the border before the second night guard arrived for his shift.

"What if you are caught by the soldiers?" Paulina worried. "There are many terrible things that could happen!" said Amelia, genuflecting. Augustina insisted "I'll be all right!" "It's the only way I can go! My mind is made up!"

Amelia embraced Augustina, placing a St. Christopher around her neck, making her promise not to take it off until she had reached her destination.

Augustina openly questioned the existence of a God who would allow their mother to be murdered and their father to live on with a new wife.

"But we have no proof they did it!" said Amelia.

"Did you expect them to confess?" asked Paulina. "Everybody knows they did it!"

They heard a noise and turned to see Heinrich in the wagon, who had come in early from the field looking like the dirty, hard-working peasant that he was. He wanted to see Augustina one more time before she left. This crazy business of her going to America was against his wishes, but now that she was of age, he could not legally stop her. And with the hostility between them, perhaps it was better for all if she went, although he did want her to come back *someday.* He got down from the wagon and approached her, managing to keep up a stern exterior. His hair looked so gray, and his shoulders were not as square as they usually were. He loved Augustina as well as all his children, yet it simply was not part of his nature to express it in words to any of them. It had been a hard life after the children's mother died, and the years since Frieda came to live at the house had taken a toll on them all.

A clattering, horse-drawn wagon pulled up containing two men in charge of taking Augustina and other hopeful passengers on their risky trip across the border. With her hands trembling, Augustina put on her babushka and tied it under her chin.

She and her brother and sisters said tearful goodbyes.

Heinrich waited beside his own wagon with Frieda who had come out of the house to anxiously join him. When Augustina and her siblings passed them carrying the roped boxes full of her selected belongings, Heinrich, trying to be stern, said goodbye and wished her good luck. Augustina almost cried, but not quite. It was clear that despite the sadness of this momentous scene, the sense of finally being free far outweighed the sentiment of saying goodbye. This was the first of many times Augustina demonstrated her ability not to allow her emotions get in the way of moving on with her life. Frieda touched her on the arm and Augustina shrank back. Frieda burst into tears and ran for the house.

Startled, Augustina looked after her, thrown off balance for an instant, then felt a rush of pity for Frieda though she didn't know why. She climbed up into the wagon. With her siblings calling emotion-filled goodbyes after her, Augustina was carried away with tears rolling down her cheeks.

It was night when the clattery horse-drawn wagon, now carrying a bulging load of hay, drew to a halt in the dark woods just inside Poland at the German border, 1907. The wagons were hidden from the sight of the two border guards about to go off duty. The two men on the driver's seat looked furtively this way and that.

Secreted in the hay in the back of the wagon were several peasants and their makeshift baggage. Augustina's babushka was tight around her head. The other frightened men, women and children crouched beside her, tensely waiting.

They whispered to each other that it must be past the hour of the change of guards. Why wasn't the wagon moving? What was going on? Had they been tricked, and their money stolen? Anxiety abounded within the wagon. One man started to peek outside to see what was happening, but another man grabbed his sleeve.

Outside on the driver's seat, the two men anxiously peered into the darkness for any sign of the bribed guard. At last they saw him hurrying to his post, telling the other guards they could go. One of the guards immediately took off, but the second lingered because his replacement was nowhere in sight.

Under the hay, the peasants felt the wagon cautiously begin to move ahead. They were relieved. All was well, and their money had not been stolen. Then the wagon abruptly stopped with a jerk, their hearts momentarily quit on them, and they struggled hard to breathe as silently as possible.

At the border, the stowaways could not see what was fearfully observed by the drivers up in the front seat. The second evening guard continued to linger, offering to stay until his replacement arrived.

The anxious wagon drivers watched until the bribed guard persuaded the evening guard that it was okay to go home.

Finally, the hidden emigrants heard the horses' hooves start up again and walk a few steps ahead.

Outside, the bribed guard, now alone, saw the hay wagon and turned his back on it and walked the other way. The driver whipped the horses into action and the freedom-seekers were carried to safety across the border to Germany.

The happy, yet, hesitant emigrants could now come out from under the hay, but their tedious trip was far from over. They would blunder about Germany which was strange to them, skimping on money, riding the train, until at last they ended up in the bustling seaport city of Antwerp, Belgium, where the ships left for America. The exhausted little group was full of mixed emotions - so relieved to have made it this far, yet so worried about what lay ahead before they could safely reach the faraway shores of their dreams.

The trees were in bloom on that Spring day upon their arrival in Antwerpen, as Augustina called the city. Amid the endless stream of passengers approaching their check-in point, as was customary, the Belgian official first addressed her in Dutch. Because she did not respond, he subsequently addressed her in French, then in German, at which point she nodded and answered his questions. The next step was passing the physical examination before being granted access to proceed on to America.

She noticed the worried look on many of her fellow passengers' faces, fearing they may not pass the exam. In the doctor's office, it was a stunning blow to Augustina to learn that her left eye, which had been bothering her for some time, did not meet the standard of health and prevented her from passing the exam. Her hopes and dreams fell apart and she broke down and cried. The sympathetic doctor explained that this did not necessarily mean she could *never* go to America. If she had an operation to correct her eye, in a year or so it might be strong enough for her to go on.

"A *year?*" lamented Augustina. "I don't have any money to pay doctors and live here for a year and still have my fare to America."

The doctor suggested that perhaps she could get a job in Antwerp and pay her way while she waited to have the operation.

Bewildered, Augustina realized that the people she started out with in the hay wagon were all going to the ship without her. Sadly, she carried her boxes by their rope handles out of the Doctor's office, not knowing where she would go.

Confused, she stood in the street, looking around helplessly. Wagons, carts and pedestrians passed her by. A large horse-drawn carriage pulled up and stopped before the building. The driver was Willem Sneiders, owner of a local boarding hotel. Sneiders regularly canvassed the immigration office looking for boarders, carrying the travelers back to his hotel to become paying guests while waiting for their ship's departure.

Augustina learned that the hotel was looking for kitchen and cleaning help, offering room, board, and a small salary. Hesitantly she spoke to Sneiders in German, explaining her plight. Willem was impressed by her honest young country looks, enhanced by her pretty, rosy cheeks and beautiful skin. He remarked that even though she was small, she looked strong and capable. He agreed to take her back to the hotel along with another prospective cleaning girl who was already aboard. Gratefully climbing into the carriage, Augustina waited while Willem collected new boarders to join them.

Augustina went to an eye doctor regularly for the next year for treatment of her 'bad' eye, whose diagnosis would culminate in surgery, which she feared may or may not resolve her problem.

During that year she met Jan - a tall, handsome 20-year-old Polish kitchen worker at the hotel. Jan noticed her right away, did her a favor by helping her pick up a heavy bag of flour, and flirted with her. Though she was shy, Augustina laughed and flirted back.

She shared with Jan about her sisters and brother, leaving out the part about Frieda and the suspicions around her father. Jan too, had been smuggled out of a different area of Poland.

He bolstered her spirit, gave her hope, made her smile. His companionship and support got her through this tough period. With his encouragement, she followed the physician's instructions faithfully, bathing her eye daily in the doctor's solution, anxiously awaiting some visible improvement in her healing process. She worked hard at the hotel amongst people of many languages, energetically cleaning, scrubbing, waiting on tables, saving every spare penny for the journey to America.

During their free hours, Augustina and Jan walked together in a beautiful nearby park and found much in common since both spoke Polish and German, and both had to delay their dream of going to America until their respective problems were solved. Jan was working diligently to replace the passage money he had lost in a card game four months before Augustina's arrival on his first night in Belgium.

Jan had learned carpentry from his father, but being too happy-go-lucky and void of any practicality, had no interest in pursuing his father's trade. He settled for an easier job in the hotel kitchen, with the idea of saving toward his replacement ticket. This turned out to be a slow process since each time he caught wind of another hot card game, he couldn't help himself, sat down at the table, and ended up losing all his money.

While he walked in the park with Augustina, he told her he had an older brother named Walter who had gone to America several months before with their uncle and two cousins. Jan was scheduled to go with them, but because he had gambled his ticket money away, they had gone on without him. Once in New York, the uncle and cousins continued on to St. Joseph, Missouri to live in a community made up of middle-European immigrants, following the advice of their neighbors back in Poland. But because he had promised to wait for Jan, Walter was still in New York working at his trade as a shoemaker. He was six years older than Jan and had come to Jan's rescue a few times before when he needed money, Jan confessed. But Walter was closely reaching his limit with his younger brother, and the truth was, he no longer was eager to bail him out.

Augustina felt that by this time she knew Jan well enough to speak her mind. She told him sternly that he might never make it to America unless he handled his money sensibly! Jan laughed that his thrifty, hard-working brother Walter had told him that same thing many times. However, being the first time he was out on his own, his love of gambling evidently was a significant part of this adventure.

"I know Walter is waiting in New York to bail me out again!" said Jan, laughing. He was confident that Walter would take him in again and try to steer him back on track, the way he had always done, contrary to Walter's recent decision against this.

Augustina challenged this, telling him if he did not change his ways, Walter would get tired of waiting in New York and go on to St. Joseph with the rest of his family. Jan threw back his head and laughed.

"I don't think so," he said. "He's pretty loyal when it comes to taking care of his little brother."

Fearing it might be a long time for her, too, if her eye didn't get better, Augustina sadly said the day might never come when she would get to America. She was ready to cry.

Jan urged her to take heart. Of course she would see America! They would get to America together! It would be more fun than going alone. He drew her close to him, telling her how much he loved her. "I want to marry you, Augustina," he declared. Her eyes widened. "Life in America will be sweet for us once we get married." Startled, Augustina's face flushed. She didn't say yes to his proposal, but she didn't say no, either. She got up and ran into the hotel. Jan smiled confidently as he looked after her.

The next time he got the chance, Jan proposed again. Why did they have to wait until they got to America? They could get married right here! Augustina's heart was a-flutter. She almost said yes, but being much more pragmatic than he, she hesitated. Jan wasn't able to hold onto enough money to support himself, let alone a wife. She thought they should at least wait until he saved up enough money and made it to America before getting married.

The trees were once again in bloom. The year was up when the doctor gave her the good news that both of her eyes were fine now – the treatment had been a success - and she could continue her journey to America. She must always be careful though, he warned, to take care of that eye.

With tears of joy filling her eyes, and adrenaline running through her veins, Augustina ran to tell Jan. She would check to see that her passport was in order, buy her third-class ticket, and set sail. There were always people leaving for America from the hotel, and she would go with the next group.

It was a terrible blow to Jan. "How can you do this to me," he wailed. Augustina sighed. "I told you over and over again that I would leave as soon as my eye was healed! I'm tired of waiting for you, Jan! Tired of being disappointed in you!"

Afraid Jan would cave into gambling again, she yelled, "Your card playing is much more important to you than I am!" He knew that she worked very hard at the hotel, was very disciplined in her spending habits, and saved every penny so she could be ready to go if and when her eye was healed.

Jan lamented that had he known her eyes would be well this soon, he would have passed up a few card games.

"*Soon*! It's been an entire year!" I've been working here and waiting for a whole year to go to America!"

He pleaded with her to loan him the passage money. When Augustina's eyes blazed angrily, he changed his plea and begged her to wait until he had enough money to pay on his own.

"I've waited long enough!" said Augustina.

She told him he was *ridiculous*. Couldn't he see he had already kept his brother Walter waiting in New York for over a year and she certainly wasn't going to fall for that trick any longer herself!

When her bags were fully packed, wearing a fresh skirt and blouse, she was ready for her departure. Chagrined Jan went to the dock with her and the other passengers in the hotel carriage, driven by Mr. Sneiders. Two people from the hotel, Rebecca and Abe, assured Jan they would take care of Augustina during the voyage. At the dock where the small ocean liner waited, Jan carried her roped boxes at a slow pace, relishing just a few more precious moments with his beloved Augustina.

Jan vowed that he would join her in the New World as soon as he could. Pressing a paper into her hand with Walter's name and New York address, he told her he'd written his brother a letter accompanied by a photograph they had taken together in the park, so Walter could identify Augustina upon her arrival in America. He told Walter he was going to marry Augustina, and asked him to meet her at the immigration station on Ellis Island. Though Jan was sure if the letter reached Walter before she arrived he would be there to meet her, Augustina worried he may not get the letter in time and she would have to experience the unknown alone. Although Augustina was incredibly strong-willed, this thought terrified her.

Jan scoffed and assured her, "Who wouldn't fall all over himself to help such a pretty girl? Whether or not Walter receives the letter, I highly doubt you would ever have to face this situation alone."

Sighing in the face of reality, he vowed that he would never gamble again. He would follow Augustina to America as soon as possible. Augustina wished she could count on that, but sincerely did not believe his plans would materialize. The ship's whistle blew as the excitement of goodbyes in a variety of languages filled the air, rising over the dock. Jan grabbed Augustina and kissed her fiercely. "So you won't forget me!" he said, blinking to hold back his tears. After her initial shock at this fervor passed, Augustina clung to him, hating to sail without him, having second thoughts about boarding her ship. Her heart pounded with anticipation, fearful of what lay ahead. As the final whistle sounded, he tore himself away from her and she boarded the ship as it cast off for the long voyage ahead. Augustina knew that the most glorious moment of her life had arrived, surpassing even her feelings for Jan, her first love. She was on her way to America.

Like a pack of animals, Augustina would say later, they were herded into third-class steerage quarters below deck on the S.S. Zeeland ship, part of the Red Star Line. The rough ocean journey began. Augustina wore Amelia's St. Christopher around her neck as she promised her older sister she would. Gazing out onto the vastness of the water, her unimaginable future lay waiting ahead.

A few hours into the voyage, as the ship tossed in a turbulent sea, passengers all around were groaning with seasickness. The heartiest ones comforted their fellow passengers heaving over the rail. Augustina almost heaved herself, but her iron will kept her from giving in. Farther along the rail, she saw Rebecca and Abe, both unable to control their nauseous stomachs.

Being so closely packed together, Augustina could not help overhear the other third-class passengers remarking about the luxuries and hoity-toity habits of the first and second-class passengers above them. They heard the music rising from the deck above, and envied that lifestyle, so far beyond anything they had ever seen in their ordinary villages. Augustina wondered what it must like to be that rich!

Several days out at sea, the passengers in third class felt the ship lurch and roll. The ship's alarm began to blare. Frightened travelers in all classes ran out on deck to find out what was wrong.

A monstrous whale was sighted in the murky Atlantic Ocean below them, swimming close to the ship. Terrified women began screaming. The crew tore into action as the alarm continued to blare. Men as well as women panicked.

Rebecca cried that the whale would turn the ship over and they would all be drowned. One terrified woman had to be carried away.

"I can't swim!" someone cried.

"Swim? Where would you swim to?"

Agitated waves lapped against the ship's sides. Augustina shrank back from the rail, staring at the gray, turbulent ocean, fearing her life was ending and they would all go down at sea. She herself had never had any occasion to learn to swim, and actually never did learn thereafter her entire life. She clutched the medallion around her neck as she knew Amelia would have wanted her to do, and felt in that moment the strength and love of her sister.

The whale was in the ship's churning wake, bumping against its side again. The ship rolled and tossed. The alarm seemed to blare louder and louder.

Then, miraculously, ships began looming up over the horizon, encircling them. First a freighter, then a British naval vessel, then other large ships forming a protective circle around their boat. As the ships' hulls began closing in on them, the giant whale disappeared under the water. The passengers were terrified it would attack from below the water line and overturn the ship. But to their dismay, the giant mammal resurfaced, blew a jet stream into the air, turned around and dove under the ocean's surface. Continuing to swim away from the ship, and much to the passengers' relief, it became a tiny speck on the horizon, then disappeared under the water's surface, taking with it any danger it had posed.

A chorus of relieved cries and sobs arose. Crewmen waved their arms in gratitude at the rescue ships and waved flags in "Thank You" signals. A woman near Augustina genuflected, thanking God for saving them. Tears flowed from Rebecca as she and several others thanked God in their own way, some out loud, some silently bowing their heads with their hands in prayer. Her husband clasped an arm around her. There was no question Augustina would now keep Amelia's medallion around her neck until at least the end of her trip. Augustina laughed with relief, hoping the worst was over.

After two weeks of more hardship than those third-class passengers could ever have expected or imagined, the ship sailed into New York Harbor without further mishap. Overjoyed, Augustina sighted the Statue of Liberty and the towering skyline of New York behind her. The sun shone down on the top of her head, lighting up her overjoyed face with a smile, as she gazed at the giant, proud statue promising a life of happiness and prosperity. Awed by the towering city in front of her, she knew not what the future held, but was certain it would be more than she could ever imagine.

The weary passengers disembarked into the confusion of Ellis Island. With the treacherous and worrisome voyage behind her and nothing but dreams and adventures ahead, Augustina, her young body supple and strong, her beautiful black eyes sparkling, her wavy brown hair flowing over her shoulders, and cheeks rosy with her inner glow, proudly, confidently, strode down the ramp, toting her cardboard boxes by their roped handles on either side. She secretly worried how she would ever find Walter among this mob of people.

Unable to speak English, she huddled in line with hundreds of other people all anxiously awaiting their turn to be cleared through Customs and the health inspections. Along with everybody else's, her makeshift luggage was untied and searched. With apprehension, she waited and watched as their hands searched her belongings among her undergarments, her other few clothes, and everything else she owned – personal and otherwise. She stood nearby anxiously waiting, looking worriedly around at the foreign surroundings that soon would become her home.

Meanwhile, Jan's older brother, Walter, with Augustina's picture in his hand, was himself anxiously searching the crowd for a face matching the one in the photograph. He was a slender Pole, nearly six feet tall, his foreign-looking clothes serviceable and neat. Like Jan, he spoke no English. In Polish, he asked a young girl if she was Augustina. She looked at him startled and shook her head, pushing her way through the crowd.

Concerned she may never find him among this mob, Augustina suddenly heard someone calling her name. She turned to see him addressing another peasant girl who smiled shyly but shook her head. Walter begged her pardon in Polish, which the girl did not understand, turning away as he continued his search.

As his hope began to fade, thinking perhaps she had not made it onto this ship, Augustina hesitantly approached him and identified herself. As happy as they were to find each other among this melee of strangers, they did not touch one other in greeting – neither a hand shake nor a hug. Walter said he had been wandering around for an hour approaching young girls asking if they were Augustina. He had all but given up. He was very impressed by how pretty she was in person and considered her a delightful surprise, but "What happened to Jan?" he asked.

They talked about his younger brother and she told him Jan did not have the passage money. "He told me he had a job," Walter stated in a puzzled tone.

"He did. He still does," said Augustina.

"What happened to the money?" he asked, then realized immediately Jan must have gambled it away. Walter shook his head in disapproval, his patience wearing thin over the troublesome habit Jan had developed in the recent years.

He told Augustina there was a vacant room in the dormitory of the rooming house where he was staying. He urged her to take it. Augustina hesitated.

"Don't worry, it's for women only," he said. "I'm in the one for men."

Augustina thought he was a godsend; if not for him, she would have no idea which way to turn in this giant, intimidating city where she could not understand one single word spoken. While there existed a striking physical resemblance, she noticed a definite difference between serious Walter's demeanor and that of his happy-go-lucky brother. Walter looked ten years older than Jan, with this mature mannerisms and polished appearance, but in reality, was only six years his senior.

Walter hoisted up her boxes with ease and took them in his charge as they traveled by streetcar to his boarding house. When Augustina tried to pay her fare, Walter insisted he already had the money out. She was grateful for his generosity, knowing her money would run out quickly. As they sat side by side on the streetcar, Augustina told him she had to find work as soon as possible to pay her way. Housework or factory, wherever they would hire someone who did not speak English. He nodded with understanding and thought she was a very fine girl with a sensible and conscientious head on her shoulders.

Augustina rented dormitory space at his rooming house, which entitled her to a bed and a cramped space to store her luggage, along with a shared bathroom down the hall. At mealtimes she and Walter ate together at a long crowded table in the noisy dining room with the other hopeful immigrants.

They walked together in Central Park. Augustina told him she used to walk in the park in Antwerpen with Jan.

"Jan wrote that you and he are going to be married," said Walter. He smiled and said he regretted this. This upset Augustina who did not know what he meant; she did not know him well enough to understand the intention in this comment. He quickly explained that he meant he wished *he* were the one marrying a beautiful and smart girl like her.

Walter told her his plans for the future. He was going to St. Joseph, Missouri in three weeks, to see about buying a shoe shop in a Middle-European settlement there. Several other family members were already there, including his uncle, who wrote and told him about the shoe shop for sale and said the owner would be willing to take a fair price. The fact that Walter spoke no English did not matter. The majority of the population there spoke Polish, German, Russian or Yiddish, and he, like so many other immigrants, knew those languages well enough to converse in, and was confident he could become fluent in those he ended up using the most.

Augustina knew all those languages herself. She said she hoped she would find a good job in New York. "Do you have to stay in New York?" asked Walter. He let her know in an unassuming manner that he was fairly well off, and told her that unlike Jan, he was a thrifty man who worked hard and saved for the day when he could buy his own business and get married. He would be *proud* to take a wife with him to St. Joseph.

"If I could find a pretty girl like you, wouldn't I be lucky?" he asked.

Augustina laughed. She thought of Jan, so young and careless with his money, and expecting her to wait for him. As tempting as it was, she knew it was not right to take up with his older brother, even though Walter was so much more responsible, the kind of man who would make a girl a good husband. Augustina loved Jan as a companion, but really couldn't see him as a reliable husband. And what if they had children? Who would be the responsible party to provide for the children? She didn't think she could depend on Jan. She found herself in a conundrum over the two brothers.

She "scratched a few lines" to her sister Amelia, and an even shorter note to Jan telling him she had arrived safely, that Walter had welcomed her, and gave him the address where she was temporarily staying.

Walter didn't have too much work piled up that day, so he impulsively asked for a few hours off so he could help Augustina settle in that afternoon. Before he arrived home to surprise Augustina, the woman who ran the boarding house had sold Augustina two pieces of paper for her letters, two envelopes, and two stamps and pointed her in the direction of the post office. This was the first time that Augustina would venture out on her own. She wore a jacket over her long dress and pinned her money to the lining in two handkerchiefs inside her corset, as her sister had taught her to do back home. Frightened, she went out in the heavy foot traffic by herself, first to the post office and then to look around and to see where she might find work.

She had been on her feet for hours and she was tired and hungry and wanted to buy a sandwich. As she unpinned one of her handkerchiefs containing part of her money, a man came up to her and smiled and spoke to her in English. She recoiled, having no idea what he said. Before she realized what was going on, he snatched the handkerchief from her hand and ran, shoving pedestrians aside, losing himself in the crowd. Augustina screamed and tried to run after him, but lost him amidst the bustling New York street.

An Irish policeman approached to help her, but he could not speak Polish. A passerby interpreted for them, then the policeman took her to the station to file a report.

Afterward, distressed, emotionally exhausted, and extremely hungry by this time, she hurried back to the boarding house. Concerned because she was gone so long and wanting to make sure she was all right, Walter had gone out looking for her. Several blocks from the house, they miraculously ran into each other. This meant so much to Augustina who was so grateful that someone cared enough to come looking for her. Walter took her back to the boarding house and told her they would meet up shortly at dinner. Famished and weary, yet very thankful, Augustina went to her room to freshen up.

The weeks went by and the only work she found was temporary kitchen help which paid very little. Her money would soon run out if her luck did not change. She received a letter from Jan about his continuing saga, trying to save enough money to come to America. As usual, his earnings from the hotel had slipped through his fingers before the next payday came.

Walter saw Augustina nearly every day. He persuaded her that it would be very difficult for a young girl who did not speak English to make it alone in New York. Walter said Jan had more or less abandoned her until he could get his wits about him and save up some money. Knowing Jan, Walter said that the temptation to gamble might delay him indefinitely, even though it was foolish of him to risk losing Augustina to someone more reliable. Like himself, for example. He took her to a secluded corner in the rooming house and opened a satchel he was carrying, making sure there was no one around to see inside it, and showed her a large amount of cash. He was eager to show it to her to make his point. She gasped, speechless as Walter proposed marriage to her then and there, waiting for an answer.

"I -- I don't know," she said, confused. She left him and hurried to line up at the bathroom to prepare for bed.

Augustina tried to sleep, but all she could do was stare up into the darkness with her heart pounding. She didn't know what to tell Walter. She was very disappointed that Jan had not arrived yet, and she was still shaken by her encounter with the thief who stole at least half of her money that she needed to live in America. She wasn't sure that she even wanted to keep on going at it alone in New York. Walter was not a bad-looking man. She reasoned that marriage to a substantial person like Walter might be the best thing that could ever happen to her! He could buy his own business, he could afford to support her, and she would not have to worry about paying her own way. And Walter trusted her. He had even opened his satchel and shown her his money!

And he was right about Jan. Even if she waited for him, there was no guarantee he would ever make it to America. He was a handsome, lovable young man but so *undependable*! If he managed to get to America someday, who knew how long it would take him to find a job? And once he got paid, who knew how long he would hold onto the money?

Augustina was afraid of the teeter-totter life Jan would give her. Which was why she did not say yes when he first asked her to marry him back in Antwerpen. He himself had told her how Walter came to his rescue many times when he got in trouble with money. It seemed that she would be the world's biggest fool to depend on him and turn stable Walter down.

Augustina's heart was torn as she tried to figure out what to do. Should she be a fool and wait for Jan, her first true love who might *never* come to America? Or should she accept Walter's offer of a solid marriage placed right in front of her? Walter was serious and dependable, he truly loved her, and she felt so *safe* with him. He certainly took away all her trepidations about her new life in America.

Walter told her he wanted to marry her in New York so he could take her to St. Joseph as his wife. She was stunned, and didn't know what to say. She stammered that she would like to see St. Joseph and the shoe shop before she made up her mind and see if she would fit in there.

Walter told her they were all immigrants in the section where the shoe shop was located and where his uncle lived. Augustina would not have to worry about learning English and she would get along fine. Everyone spoke his own language there.

When he couldn't change her mind, he became impatient. He managed to hold his temper though, and he finally agreed to buy her a train ticket to go with him to see the shop.

They said goodbye to New York and boarded the train and settled in their coach seats. Augustina was sick with guilt about Jan.

CHAPTER FOUR

Walter and Augustina arrived in St. Joseph late on a Saturday evening. Walter said it was too late to disturb his uncle. They would have to wait and see him in the morning. Looking very much like the immigrants they were, with their combined rope-tied cardboard boxes and Walter's large once-nice-but-now-battered suitcase that was beginning to show wear, they set out on foot to find a rooming house. They found one near the train station, where Walter rented separate rooms for them. Augustina realized he was spending a lot of money on her and she worried. She was tired, but she tossed and turned before she fell asleep. She worried that Walter might want some of his money back if she didn't stay.

The next morning, after each finishing a cup of coffee and a roll in a nearby restaurant, Walter inquired what streetcar would take them to his uncle's house. Following the directions written on a small piece of paper, they made their way to the street and house number, toting all their clumsy luggage, surprising his family with a knock on the door. Augustina and Walter were greeted with shock. Though Walter had sent a letter ahead saying they were coming, his relatives hadn't yet received it.

Augustina met the uncle and his wife, his wife's mother, and her sister, all living together in the house. They were taken aback to meet his pretty young companion when they learned her name was Augustina. Walter proudly told them that he was going to marry her. The uncle's wife said Jan had written them and said he had a girl named Augustina. Augustina exchanged a guilty glance with Walter.

Walter confirmed that it was the same Augustina, but *he* was going to marry her instead. The relatives were shocked to hear this, particularly the uncle's wife. Jan was their favorite. Walter was always so serious and stern, while Jan lived a light-hearted life, was more fun to be around, and always made them laugh. In no uncertain terms, the aunt made it clear that she considered Augustina a hussy.

Augustina was allowed to go with Walter and his uncle to see the shoe shop. The owner of the shoe shop, a Russian Jew, showed them around his store. They went upstairs to the apartment located above the shop, and off a long hallway, found a kitchen, a combination bedroom and living room, and a room which served as a pantry, service porch and storage. The present owner had lived there with his wife and two children for 9 years. Walter was immediately pleased with what he saw, could already imagine the two of them living here, yet tried not to appear too anxious because he wanted to get the price down.

Being an educated and savvy businessman, he was clear on what he wanted and ready to close the deal. He told Augustina to wait in the living room with his uncle and the others while he and the owner went downstairs to discuss business. A short while later a fair and just agreement was reached followed by a solid handshake and plans to draw up papers in preparation for the final signatures.

Meanwhile, Augustina sat in the apartment living room with the owner's family, saying very little. She understood some Yiddish from the Old Country, but she certainly was not comfortable making conversation and sharing her feelings with these strangers from whom she was not feeling much warmth or compassion.

When later that evening Walter told Augustina he had sealed the deal, though she said nothing, she silently decided it would be the right choice to pick Walter over Jan.

Walter hired a Polish Jew lawyer who lived in the neighborhood to review the papers and protect his interests. Augustina was impressed by how smart the lawyer was. Though her relationship with Jan was a difficult one to let go of completely, Walter's demonstration of a solid business sense confirmed her intuition it was foolish to give up a good man like Walter. Marriage was not a light-hearted card game to laugh and joke about and drag your family around to suffer your unnecessary losses with you. She made her decision to move to St. Joe, as everyone called the city, and marry Walter before a Justice-of-the-Peace, despite her lingering guild over Jan.

Walter's uncle, along with the shoemaker and his wife, stood up for the couple as witnesses. Because Jan was a favorite with his family, the other relatives wanted no part of this wedding. Augustina was relieved, for having them there with curled lips and accusing eyes staring disapprovingly at her during the ceremony would have turned her own special wedding day into a miserable one. Instead, it was simple, yet joyous afternoon for the new bride.

Walter happily took over his duties as the new shoemaker in town, while Augustina cleaned, cooked and washed clothes by hand on a scrub board in their upstairs home. Abiding by the prominently accepted belief that men were inherently superior to women and the man was always to be looked up to, Augustina unquestioningly respected her strict, thrifty husband, confident that he would always provide her with the security and guidance a faithful wife needed.

Sometimes she went downstairs to the shoe shop and watched Walter hammering soles onto shoes, holding his iron shoe last between his knees to steady his fastidious work. He was a good shoemaker, a good provider, and certainly a good man at his core.

Though not amounting to a great deal, money came in steadily from the middle-European immigrants of the area who always had rubber heels and leather soles to mend. Walter was very thrifty and Augustina never argued nor questioned having to scrimp, for she knew it meant security for the both of them.

She soon became acquainted with some of the neighbors who also lived above their shops on the block. Anna, a buxom German-Jewish housewife in her late twenties who lived a few doors down, befriended her at once. She had two children, ages six and eight, and Anna quickly became Augustina's closest friend. On weekends and sometimes during the week after dinner, she and her husband, Hans, made home brew in a crock and shared it with Augustina and Walter, enhancing their friendship. Anna became very helpful and protective toward the younger Augustina, and did not like one bit the way Walter's family treated his new bride.

Anna helped her friend learn Yiddish more fluently, for there were many Jews living among them. This meant that although Augustina had little formal education, she could now comfortably speak the popular four languages of the region - Polish, German, Russian and Yiddish - easing the strain of not fitting in that she had carried with her from Poland and giving her for the first time confidence in herself and her social skills.

However, the heavy resentment toward Walter's wife continued to emanate from the family each time they saw Augustina. The friction was so thick that Augustina found herself avoiding his family at all costs. Her excuses were becoming more and more frequent, and she feared the tension building up inside might actually make her sick.

On a cold November day less than a year later, Augustina made Walter a very happy man. As she cleaned the rooms in her home above the shoe shop, Augustina felt her first contraction, and soon went into labor. A neighbor ran to his horse and buggy to fetch the doctor. Walter attempted to maintain an authoritative air as he gave commands, but truthfully, had no idea what to do. Anna, her wits collected, entered the room calmly and effectively helped with the delivery.

Augustina's small bones and 5"1" frame made for a challenging delivery. The baby, weighing nearly 9 pounds, posed a challenge as he came through the birth canal. The doctor had no alternative but to use forceps. As she felt her body ripping, she screamed in terror. After several long minutes, the doctor successfully delivered their first-born son, weighing a healthy eight pounds, twelve ounces, whom they named Sigmond. That evening, when it was all over, she lay in bed, sweaty, her face tear-streaked, holding this amazing little bundle in her arms. She tried not talk too much about, nor burden Walter with her painful ordeal, for she knew that was just one of the many things all women had to go through.

It was quite a workout for the doctor, as well. After he washed up, the doctor congratulated Walter. Augustina lovingly cuddled the child, and with Anna's help, tried to nurse little Sig. Beaming, Walter pulled up a bed sheet to shield Augustina's bare breast from the others in the room and exclaimed, "There is nothing so fine as having a first-born son!"

After the doctor packed up his bag and left, Anna shooed the others out so she could give Augustina some tips to help her nurse her baby. Walter happily went back downstairs to catch up on his work. Alone with Anna and the baby, Augustina clumsily finished nursing, set the sleeping baby beside her, then unleashed a flood of tears and pent-up emotions on Anna's sympathetic ear.

A make-shift cradle was provided for little Sigmond, and Walter set it up beside their bed.

When Augustina gained back her strength, Anna helped her write a few lines to Amelia and told her to tell everyone about the baby Sigmond, making sure to pass the good news to Gottlieb and little Maria. Her writing was barely legible, and her spelling was worse, but they had managed to make out the gist in the letters she had sent in the past. Now, with the help of Anna, she was sure they would be able to receive her good news.

Augustina laughed. "Won't they be surprised it's a boy! I wish I could see Maria's face when Amelia reads her the letter."

But a return letter from Amelia informed her that when the cold set in that winter, their little sister Maria had died of pneumonia. Augustina's shock and sadness was almost inconsolable. Walter was sympathetic for a while, but finally spoke sharply to her, urging her to pay more attention to taking care of "the boy!"

In the following days, the only thing that could distract Augustina from her grief was when Sigmond cried out to her from his cradle, and she hurried over to nurse him and tend to his needs.

Understanding her grief, Anna helped her get through this terrible time. Not yet twenty years old, Augustina listened well to her immigrant friend's advice on child care and home remedies. She learned how to "doctor" herself and her child, as well as Walter when necessary, to cure infections by bathing the afflicted area in hot water, to give or take "physics" to make sure they all got cleaned out internally every day, to get plenty of sleep, eat sensibly, have hot nourishing soup often, and tend to Sigmond's childhood illnesses with devoted care.

Walter's relatives still gave Augustina a hard time. They never let her forget that she "played a dirty trick" on Jan, the family's favorite, by marrying Walter. They never let Walter forget it either, but they visibly placed more of the blame on Augustina with their rude and blatant behavior.

When the boy was old enough to toddle around the house, Augustina began to grow restless and longed to learn more about America. Without knowing much English, and remembering what had happened to her on her first day out alone in New York, she dared not wander farther than her immediate neighborhood.

Anna, who could speak some English, told Augustina there was a night school not too far away where immigrants could go to learn the language and study to become citizens. It was only two nights a week, and the school was *free*! Anna herself had gone there for a semester. Augustina didn't know what a semester was, but she was excited to hear about it.

She pleaded with Walter to let her go to night school and learn English. It was free! He was shocked and thought she undoubtedly was joking. She laughed and said, "No! It really is free!" Surely he would not mind if she went two nights a week to a free school after the boy was asleep. Walter shouted at Augustina, enraged to think she would want to leave the boy! Augustina emphasized *only* after he was asleep! "Anna said the school is only ten or twelve blocks away! It will be easy to walk there. And it's free - it won't cost anything!"

"I don't want Anna to put notions like that in your head!" stormed Walter. He demanded to know why Augustina wanted to waste her time that way! She belonged at home taking care of the boy! They didn't need English where they lived! Didn't she have a husband who provided a good living for her and the boy?

"Anna is trying to start something, putting such nonsense in your head! I don't speak English and I've never needed it! When there are papers to sign, I go to my lawyer, don't I? Like the legal papers when I bought this shop. The lawyer took care of everything!"

Opposing her husband, Augustina repeated that she wanted to go to night school. She would learn to write letters to her sisters and understand Americans when they talked, to read signs and American newspapers, and understand how to raise her child 'the American way.'

Walter said she already could write letters to her sisters! What more did she want? He did not want her to wear herself out going to school when she had plenty to do taking care of the house, cooking, and raising the boy.

Once again, Augustina's stubbornness rose to the surface. Why *shouldn't* she learn English? Would it hurt Walter? Anna could walk to school with her the first night and help her get signed up.

Walter grew red with anger. He feared that Augustina would get new ideas in her head that would make her restless and independent of him. In his eyes, schooling was a threat to their marriage.

And for the second time in her life, Augustina's determination to fight for her education until she won the battle, came forth with fervor. She persuaded Walter to let her go for one night to see what it was like. So, the next night, Augustina put little Sigmond to sleep in the new cradle Walter had bought when the boy became too big for his first bed, and got ready to go to school. Walter argued with her, but she was adamant. She ran out into the hall to wait for Anna to come and accompany her on her first night of school in America.

Anna didn't dare go into their apartment, as she knew how angry Walter was, blaming her for his wife's desire to become educated and more independent. She stood outside the door with a long face and the bad news that Hans, her husband, had forbidden her to accompany Augustina to school because it would cause such hard feelings with Walter. She pulled Augustina down the hall so Walter couldn't hear and gave her careful directions on how to get to school, then hurried back to her room. Augustina took a deep breath, checked on the boy once again to make sure he was asleep, refused to look angry Walter in the eye, and left.

Feeling as though she were running away from home, tears filled her eyes as she started down the street.

The first night at citizenship school was a glorious but intimidating experience. Trying to ignore the deep-seated feelings of guilt because of Walter's anger at her being there in the first place, she focused on the teacher, the desks and chairs, and the other students. Seated next to her was a Russian woman named Olga, who helped her get through the evening. The two women became friends and thereafter sat together. Augustina picked up a few words of English that first evening, but continued using select words such as 'yah' from her native tongue and childhood years in Poland.

A few weeks later when she came home from school, Walter was impatient with her, complaining that the boy didn't want to go to sleep without her, and when he finally did, he would wake up crying out for her. "We need you at home!" cried Walter. Augustina begged him to have a little more patience for the few hours she was away.

But after several weeks, little Sigmond came down with a bad stuffy cold that kept him crying incessantly. One evening when Augustina went to school, he woke up screaming and gasping, barely able to catch his breath. Walter was frantic. He ran down the hall to seek Anna's help. Anna came running and with one of her faithful home remedies, settled and soothed little Sigmond so they did not have to fetch a doctor. Walter was so relieved he almost cried. Then he remembered that it was Anna's fault that his wife was not home to care for her child. What if Anna hadn't been home to help Sigmond? Grudgingly, he thanked her, but vowed there would be no more emergencies like this, because Augustina would be home where she belonged!

When Augustina came home, he shouted that she would go to school *no more*! She must stay home where she belonged and take care of the boy! Augustina was aghast when she heard what happened. She ran to Sigmond's crib to make sure he was still breathing. She wanted to pick him up and cradle him in her arms, but Walter pulled her away, whispering frantically "Don't wake him." Augustina knew that if anything happened to her baby when she was at school, she would never get over it. With a sinking heart, she moved slowly away from the boy's bed. In the next room, she told Walter that he was right. She must never leave her baby again.

The next day, a resigned Augustina was washing clothes on her scrubbing board with strong, pungent Peet Laundry Soap, her household cleaning agent. It made the hands rough and red, but housewives didn't have much of an alternative. The windows upstairs were open and she could hear Walter downstairs hammering soles and heels on shoes and banging about in the shop. Tears filled her eyes. She was helpless – she saw only two alternatives – go to school or take care of her son. She had to do what she knew was right deep down inside.

Anna came looking for her. She was sorry Augustina had to quit school, but lovingly reminded her that maybe one day in the future, she could go back.

Augustina shook her head, declaring that she never would. It had always been this way. First, her father forbade it, now her husband. She was a wife and mother now, and she had more important things to attend to than school.

Chapter Five

Jan finally made it to America. In spite of his vow not to go to St. Joseph and face such awkward circumstances, he went anyway. The baby, Sigmond, was now two years old. As soon as Jan found out where Walter and Augustina lived, he headed over to confront them.

Through the front window, Jan saw Walter at work in the shoe shop downstairs. Jan managed to sneak up the back stairs without being seen. He knocked on the upstairs door and caught Augustina off-guard cleaning house. With no idea that he was in town, she was dumbfounded. She blocked the doorway to keep him from coming in, but he persuaded her to step aside and open the door. The boy was playing on the floor. Jan had heard from his relatives that they had had a baby, but actually seeing the little boy was more hurtful to Jan than he could have imagined. He still did not get the correlation between his irresponsible lifestyle and Augustina's decision to marry Walter. An emotionally charged confrontation ensued.

"You were supposed to wait for me!" he stormed at her.

"I told you over and over, I couldn't depend on you!" she retorted.

Jan could only remember how perfect things were with them in Antwerp. He said, "I should never have sent Walter to meet you! Well now I've come to take you away from Big Brother!" Augustina reached out to take Sigmond from the room, but Jan grabbed her by the shoulders, pulling her close to him, and began kissing her passionately.

Walter walked in and could not believe the scene before his eyes. Augustina was struggling to get away, but Walter couldn't tell if she still had any feelings for Jan. He ordered her to take the boy and get out of the room. Quickly she did as she was told.

Jan had the audacity to try to shake hands with Walter, but Walter wouldn't have any of it. He hauled off and punched Jan in the jaw as hard as he could, sending him reeling across the room.

"Get out of my house!" he shouted, "You're not welcome around here!" Rubbing his throbbing jaw and glaring at Walter, Jan staggered out.

The following day, Jan showed up at the shoe shop and tried to borrow money from Walter, who could hardly believe what his brother was requesting of him. Jan said Walter owed him plenty. He stole Augustina. Their voices rose in anger. Walter pointed out that if Jan were not such a gambler, Augustina might have married him before Walter ever met her.

Bitter, Jan bad-mouthed both Walter and Augustina to his uncle and cousins and their spouses. Swayed by Jan's version of the story, they sided with him more than ever. This caused even a greater rift between Augustina and Walter's family that never healed.

One morning in 1914 when Augustina was walking Sigmond to kindergarten, they saw a newsboy waving a newspaper for all to see, shouting, "Extra!" Augustina could understand a few words the newsboy was saying. She was shocked and fearful for her family in Poland. English-speaking immigrants on the street huddled with excitement, talking in their respective languages about the war that had just erupted in Europe. Augustina gasped. She, like most of them, had family in the Old Country.

As the war spread to Poland, Walter worried about his parents in Warsaw, and Augustina worried about her two remaining sisters, Paulina and Amelia, their brother, Gottlieb, and others back home that she cared about. She even worried about her father and stepmother Frieda, but then she supposed they could take care of themselves as they had done so thus far.

Walter and the neighbors talked about the war with very strong opinions, but Augustina, except for what she heard, knew nothing of the geography, nor the politics, nor the situation, nor the positions of the powers involved. The one thing she clearly heard people saying was, "The Germans started it!" Many of the immigrants turned against all Germans without knowing whose side the individuals were on in the war. When they looked accusingly at Augustina, she felt their sting and became angry and defensive, for she felt there was not one German in all of America more innocent in this matter than Augustina.

A letter finally arrived from Amelia. The brother Gottlieb and all the young men in their town, including Amelia's and Paulina's husbands, had been taken to the war against the Germans. Amelia wrote that the shelling in nearby areas had left many dead, many homeless, many forced to move away to remove themselves from the encroaching war.

"The Army stands at Riga," Amelia wrote. "We can hear the guns coming closer and closer." Paulina and her family had already left to stay with friends in Russia. The address of the friend was at the bottom of the letter with a note saying Paulina wanted Augustina to write. Her father, Heinrich and her stepmother, Frieda, had left for her sister's house in another part of Poland where the war had not yet spread. Amelia and her children were packing up that very day to go stay with a distant cousin out of range of the firing. Amelia wrote the cousin's address in the letter.

With worry and fear, Augustina "scratched a few lines" to both Amelia and Paulina. It was a horribly devastating time for the immigrants in America who had relatives left in Europe, and of course for the Europeans themselves in the thick of the war.

Back in St. Joe, Jan got a job as a waiter and continued to gamble. He rented a room near his relatives, which made it convenient for him whenever he wanted to borrow money. He was exhilarated when he won at the gambling tables, and not too worried when he lost, for his family could usually be persuaded to make sure he was taken care of until he got his next week's pay.

For all his strength and dominance, Walter was concerned because, not only was he several years older than Augustina, but with her petite stature, energetic mannerisms, and rosy cheeks, she looked a lot younger than her actual years. Even though Augustina continued to ignore Jan, in Walter's mind, his younger brother was a constant threat. When it came to girls, Jan usually got the one he had his eye on.

Then one day out of the blue, Jan decided he wanted to help beat the Germans. He studied and passed his citizenship test, then enlisted in the United States Army. When he was sent overseas, Walter and Augustina were glad he wouldn't be bothering them for a while, however much they worried about his safety in the war.

In 1917 after America joined World War One, Augustina and Anna talked about the heartbreak of the disappearance of Augustina's family. She never received a reply from her last letter. Augustina was certain that in the turmoil of the war-torn land, they had lost her address, if indeed they had managed to survive. Later, she would sit in the dark alone with a hot toddy, brooding over this and wondering, wondering, wondering whatever became of her family, a resolution that never came.

Sigmond was now a handsome nine year old boy, doing well in school. Augustina wanted to learn to read better, and she often sat with the boy when he did his lessons, asking him about words in his reading book. She pointed to each word as they read, and he told her what it was. She was delighted. She still looked at the newspaper every day and tried to make out the words, but help from Sigmond was always welcomed.

One day when Walter came upstairs from the shoe shop to eat his lunch, Augustina brought up the subject of going to school again. The answer was a flat NO. Normally she bowed to all his wishes, but this time a heated argument arose. Walter gulped down his lunch and stomped out of the apartment, slamming the door.

It was six o'clock in the evening and they usually had supper at five. Augustina had a pot of steaming stew on the stove ready to serve and had grown impatient because Walter had not yet come home. She went downstairs and found the shop closed, which puzzled her. She went back upstairs and knocked on Anna's door. Hans answered, also surprised that Walter had not yet come upstairs. He said Walter closed up the shop early, telling him that he needed to pick up some leather for the next day's work. Irritated, Augustina thought he could have waited until tomorrow to go after the leather.

Sigmond was a growing boy, always hungry, so she dished up his food. He was wolfing it down when they heard a knock at the door. Augustina opened it and found Hans standing there, his face white. Anna stood behind him with a stunned look on her face. Hans motioned for Augustina to send the boy from the room. Her worried eyes sought his and those of Anna. Sigmond had practically finished eating what was on his plate, so Augustina handed him a plate with a piece of her home-made cake and sent him out of the room. Her heart was racing. She knew the news must be bad.

"What's happened to Walter?" she asked, her voice trembling.

Hans looked at her with great pity. Walter, he said, had just left his leather supplier and was walking along the railroad tracks a few blocks south, when a train struck and killed him.

Augustina screamed as she went into shock. Sigmond came running back into the room. Anna and Hans helped her to the couch where she lay down, screaming and sobbing.

Walter had been identified by a man who recognized him as one of the shoemakers in their neighborhood.

Anna and Hans were there to help Augustina through the terrible days ahead. Augustina could not forget that the last words she and her husband exchanged took the form of a heated debate over the subject of Augustina going back to school. That evening as he walked beside the railroad tracks, his mind must have been on this argument. In tears, Augustina reasoned that if he hadn't been so worried and distracted, he would have heard the train's whistle and gotten off the tracks.

That night, she heard the train's shrill whistle in a nightmare. It was very dark in her dream, and she was running in front of the train, terrified, stumbling on the track, afraid she would fall. The train was about to hit her when she woke up screaming.

Walter's relatives attended the funeral, looking at Augustina accusingly and giving the widow little support.

Walter's Polish lawyer came to Augustina's home to talk to her about Walter's estate. Augustina told the attorney she did not want to live among Walter's hostile relatives any longer. They did everything they could think of to make her life miserable. She wanted to sell the shoe shop, take the boy and get away from St. Joseph! In the back of her mind she wondered if Kansas City would be the right choice, as Hans and Anna often praised that city.

She was told by the lawyer that she had to wait a year until the estate was settled with the money from the shoe shop and other money from Walter's accounts. Being a frugal man, Walter had accumulated an impressive savings. The lawyer explained that Walter's creditors needed time to come forth and claim anything he owed. Augustina protested that everybody knew Walter always paid cash. He was an honest man, and did not owe anyone. The court, however, had to make that decision, ensuring his record was clean and all debts paid before dispersing any monies to his beneficiaries.

The grieving young widow now had the task of trying to find enough money to support herself and her son until Walter's estate was settled. Anna and Hans were worried about Augustina's plan to go alone with the child to Kansas City to get away from the relatives who blamed her for all the terrible things that were happening. Anna advised her to see if she could find a job in the meantime. It would help her support herself and the boy, save a little money, and take her mind off her sorrow. Anna graciously offered to take care of Sigmond after school until Augustina got home from work. Anna said it would be a pleasure, because Sig got along well with her youngest boy just a bit older than Sigmond, and it would make it easier on her as well.

"How can I get a job?" Augustina questioned. She still could barely understand or speak English.

Anna assured her that it did not matter. She could look for a factory job. Many girls working in the factories could not speak English. She urged her to give it a try. Anna would help her find places to look, and supervise Sigmond in her absence.

Augustina found a job dipping chocolate in a candy factory, working on a line along with several other immigrant and American girls.

One young girl stood out from all the rest, a beautiful young woman named Kristine who worked next to Augustina on the assembly line. Kristine was vivacious, smiled a lot and was always friendly and helpful to Augustina.

"She's the prettiest girl I ever saw!" Augustina told Anna.

But not all the women were that kind to Augustina. With the war in full swing and people's hardened beliefs and attitudes openly exhibited toward Germans, some of her coworkers looked at her and other German girls as though they personally started the war. They sneered at her, as Augustina put it, blaming her personally for the hell that was taking place over there, and for the lives that were lost, when, in fact, she had no idea what the War was all about. When she told the girls that, they snapped, "I don't care what you say you *know or don't know*! You're German!"

Augustina snapped back, "I was only in Germany ONE DAY in my entire life. I didn't have time to start the war!"

At home, she told Anna, "Those women have never been *any place* and they don't know *anything*!" Anna agreed with her.

Augustina's work wasn't easy. The hours were long and the pay was short, but Augustina did not question it. She and the other girls could eat all the chocolates they wanted as long as they did not try to stuff any in their pockets and take it home. Oh, how Augustina enjoyed the unlimited candy – at first! Then, like the other girls, she soon got tired of it and the excitement wore off.

When the year was up, Augustina attended a legal hearing and Walter's estate was settled. Augustina received several thousand dollars from the sale of the shoe shop as well as Walter's savings accumulated throughout his life. Walter's relatives begrudged Augustina's inheritance. The uncle's wife said it worked out conveniently well for Augustina. "She married Walter so she could inherit more money than if she had married Jan!"

When the war was over and Jan returned home, Augustina would have nothing to do with him. He pestered her for a while, then gave up and turned his attention to other pretty girls who were happy to have a handsome man chasing after them.

Augustina could not wait to take the boy to Kansas City and get away from this terrible bunch. She had been told that Kansas City was all the way across the state of Missouri and much bigger than St. Joe. She was eager to go, but frightened to think of arriving with her boy to another strange place. There, she would *have* to speak English, a language she barely could pronounce, with the responsibility of a boy to support. But once again, opportunity beckoned. Although she had not yet gotten her citizenship papers, because Sigmond was born in America, he was naturally a U.S. Citizen. She thought it was a good choice to give her son the chance to grow up with more American children than he would have in their immigrant community in St. Joe.

CHAPTER SIX

Their train pulled into the Kansas City station, and toting her cumbersome baggage and nine-year-old Sigmond, Augustina disembarked. Standing on the platform, they looked around at their strange new surroundings. Augustina, a slender, pretty, petite young lady with a full bosom and rosy cheeks, stood very straight, lending great importance to her five-foot-one stature. She looked much younger – closer to twenty years old - than her actual twenty-eight years.

As she made her way along the street with her boy and their clumsy cardboard boxes and bulging old suitcase, she was fearful of what strangers might do if they knew of the bank draft she carried. She had tied up her cash in two handkerchiefs inside the top of her corset, being extra cautious as she thought about how the pickpocket in New York had stolen half of her life's savings.

Augustina went directly to a Kansas City bank with a large sign that made it appear to her both legitimate and trustworthy, where she deposited the bank draft into an account. She cautioned Sigmond not to tell *anyone* about this transaction.

They found the Kansas City of that era a city of street cars, horse-drawn ice wagons, milk wagons, shouting hucksters peddling their wares from their wagons, and a few automobiles driving down the streets.

Street sweepers walked in the boulevards pushing their trash barrels ahead of them, cleaning the streets with long-handled push brooms. Ridding the roads of horse manure comprised most of their work.

Augustina rented a kitchenette above a store in downtown Kansas City, on a business street called Troost Avenue. She was happy that a streetcar ran right by the building, making transportation easy for them. She enrolled the boy in a grammar school within walking distance. It was a neighborhood where Americans and immigrants lived side by side and nearly everybody spoke English.

Augustina found a job in a downtown tailor shop seven blocks away, where she could walk to work. Jews from the Old Country, who knew Polish and German as well as she did, owned the tailor shop. They taught her to make alterations on men's clothing. She was pleased to be earning money again. The wages were low and she worked long hours six days a week, as was the custom. The boss was a lecher which meant she constantly had to keep a watchful eye out for and avoid being the target of any inappropriate behavior. For a year, Augustina worked very hard under these conditions, with little time for pleasure.

She worried about Sigmond staying by himself after school until she got home from work at suppertime. She told him to lock the door and not let any strangers in! He was an obedient boy who so far had not gone out looking for mischief, and she hoped he would stay that way.

Sigmond had a few tough times adjusting to the ways of the American schoolboy, because his whole life in St. Joseph was spent surrounded by Old Country customs and languages. His adjustment was made all the more difficult when a big bully in his class kept calling him a Pollock. Spoiling for a fight, the bully knocked him down one day on the way home from school. Though never having fought anyone before, when the bully towered over him with his fists clenched, Sig scrambled to his feet and began throwing wild punches. He got in one or two good licks that the bully would not soon forget. Sig scooped up his book from the sidewalk with its wrinkled, dirty pages, and ran for his life.

Augustina was frightened when she saw one of his eyes all red and swollen, his face bruised, his damaged schoolbook, and his clothes a dirty mess. Angry about what had happened to him, she was also upset about the desecration of the precious school book. Without a husband or male role model, she didn't know how to handle the bully. To Augustina's great relief, a boy in Sig's class named Willard, who was a little taller and huskier than Sig, saw what had happened and from that day forward stuck up for him. Together they faced the bully down and he never bothered Sig again. Sig and Willard became fast friends and built a friendship lasting for years beyond high school.

At home in the evenings, Augustina mended and ironed her own clothes and those of the boy. She repaired their shoes by buying rubber heels and soles from the dime store and nailing and gluing them onto the old shoes, using Walter's iron shoemaker's last.

But the most important thing of all as far as Augustina was concerned, outside of raising her child, was that she was learning to read and understand the English language better. Her speech, however, was still hard for an American to understand. The sound 'th' was the hardest – the word 'this' became 'dis' and 'thing' became 'ting.' Her attempts at reading the daily newspaper were beginning to pay off as she was able to make out more and more words more frequently. She said the words out loud as best she could when she read the paper while running her finger along the lines. Often, she guessed the words wrong and Sig corrected her. At first, her English was almost impossible to understand, but if a sympathetic listener focused with just a little more effort than usual, they could usually make out at least part of what she was saying.

With the boy's help, she laboriously ran her forefinger along the printed lines of the Kansas City Star, the morning newspaper that she looked forward to reading each day, and when she could afford it, she also bought the Kansas City Journal, the afternoon newspaper. When important news broke at other times of the day, paperboys could be heard shouting, "Extra! Extra! Read all about it!" Many people ran to buy that special edition newspaper but Augustina had to hear what happened from talk on the street if she didn't understand the headlines, as she certainly could not afford to buy any more papers.

One spring day as she and the other employees were leaving work, her boss called her into his office and shut the door. He waited until all the other employees had gone, then backed her into a corner and tried to kiss her. She twisted away from him and ran for the door. He shouted that if she told anyone, he would fire her. When she ran out the door, he slammed it after her.

Full of despair, she was walking down a street on her way home, a street she had walked many times before, with her head hanging low, crying. Suddenly she noticed a HOUSE FOR SALE sign nailed to a stick in front of a two-story brick house that had always been one of her favorites on her route home. Two smaller signs tacked to one of the round wooden posts that held the roof up over the front porch, read: ROOM FOR RENT and GARAGE FOR RENT. Drawn in by the beautiful flowers in the front yard, she paused and carefully looked the place over. She guessed it had been built about 30 years ago. A circle of bricks in the center of a patchy grass yard enclosed a flourishing crop of roses and tall red hollyhocks, whose fragrance reached her nostrils. Gorgeous pink and white morning glories climbed a trellis at the right side of the porch, with fragrant mint growing alongside. The narrow driveway consisted of brown and green grass with two cracked cement strips the width of a car's tires along either side. The other side of the property was bordered by blue irises. She stood transfixed, gazing at the house in all its glory. Walking by this house many times, it had never looked so beautiful, and she never dreamed that this house would someday be up for sale.

The front yard was enclosed by a wire fence about three feet high. A gate swung inward to the cement walk that led to the house. On the front porch, a comfortable-looking wooden swing was attached by chains to the porch roof. The driveway led to two frame garages in the rear with corrugated tin roofs.

Augustina wanted to stop and ask to see the inside of the house, but she hesitated to confront strangers alone with her broken English that most Americans could not understand. Besides, it was suppertime. They were probably eating. She hurried to get home and tell the boy!

She was flushed and happy when she told the boy about the house. Sig had not seen the house with the sign up, and Augustina had to describe it in detail before he understood which one she was referring to.

All that evening she thought about the house. It would be a good rooming house in a good location. She tried to explain to Sig that if she could buy a place like that with the money his father left, she could make a living and have a real home for them. She could stop paying out all that rent money for the little kitchenette the way she was doing now, and start getting some return on her money. Working in her own house, she would always be there when the boy came home from school. To herself, she thought, if she could make ends meet, it would beat working at the tailor shop and fighting off the boss.

The next Sunday afternoon, her first day off work since she had seen the house, she showed up at the front door with the boy to help with the translation.

When she pinched the doorbell handle and turned it clockwise, a loud raking ring resounded throughout the house. A few minutes later, a middle-aged woman answered the door wearing a print kitchen apron over her dress, her gray hair pulled back in a knot at the nape of her neck. Looking them over quickly, she asked, "Yes?"

Augustina said, as best she could, "We see your house is for sale." The woman could not understand her accent. Augustina turned to Sigmond, who repeated her statement clearly. The aproned woman thought Augustina looked too young to be talking about buying a house without having her father or husband with her.

"My father died and my mother wants to look at the house," said Sigmond.

"This is your *mother*?" asked the woman in surprise. She told Augustina she looked more like the boy's sister. Augustina chuckled and shook her head.

"Do you want to rent a room?" asked the woman.

With the boy's help, Augustina told her, "No, I want to buy the house. How much you want for it?"

The surprised woman shrewdly looked her over.

"Ten thousand dollars," she said.

Augustina looked startled. It took a moment for her to answer. "That's a lot of money," she said. She stepped back and didn't say anything for a while. Her heart was pounding.

The woman watched her, then started to close the door.

"I want to look at the place," said Augustina as best she could. The woman did not understand. Sigmond repeated his mother's wishes.

She looked at Augustina with uncertainty. "You mean you want to *buy* this house?"

Augustina nodded. "Yah," she said.

The woman hesitated, looking from one to the other. "My husband's not home right now, but I suppose I could show it to you. She stood aside so they could come in. "I'm Mrs. Soxmen. My husband is the owner."

Augustina and Sigmond stepped into the hallway where a staircase with worn woolen flowered carpeting and a wooden banister led to the second floor. Sigmond had to interpret for Augustina several times in Polish so the women could understand one another.

"Me and my husband live back here," said the woman. She led them to the rear of the hallway, through a door with a glass window in the upper part and a white lace curtain on the inside.

It led to four rooms which the owners used as living quarters. Light bulbs were hanging from wires from the ceiling, and Augustina noticed the large ice box off the kitchen. The house had wooden floors with patterned area rugs, some of them frayed. Some rooms had linoleum on the floor, as the owner's own living room did. "It's easier to keep clean," she said.

The patterned wall-papered rooms were light and airy, with high ceilings and tall casement windows. Augustina and her boy were ushered through a narrow entrance room with a daybed and a vanity dresser; a large, light living room with sunlight streaming through a transom over a side door with a small porch outside that overlooked the driveway, and a small bedroom that had been added on to the original house. The large kitchen had a black iron stove with round removable iron lids on the top to cook on and to stuff coal or wood inside for burning. A round dining table surrounded by five mismatched straight chairs with carved backs and spindles sat on the other side of the room.

Pleased, Augustina looked around, nodding. The woman opened a door from the kitchen and snapped on a light switch inside. Warning them to hold onto the wooden railing, she led them down a narrow dim stairway to the basement. A bare light bulb hung on an electric cord suspended from the basement ceiling.

They found themselves in a large cellar that included a furnace and a high window that opened from two hinges at the top and looked outside at ground level.

"They dump the coal for the furnace through that window," explained Mrs. Soxmen.

Augustina turned to the boy for an explanation. "In the wintertime," he clarified.

Old trunks and boxes stood against the wall on one side of the basement, and stacked up against another wall were columns of jars of preserves, peaches, and other home canned goods.

"There's plenty of room here for your canning," said Mrs. Soxmen.

Augustina nodded, thinking that besides that there was also enough room between the musty-smelling walls to put in a crock of home brew, the way Anna and Hans did.

Mrs. Soxmen took them upstairs again and out the back door of the kitchen. Patches of grass sprang up in the back yard between patches of dirt, and a trash pile stood in the middle of the yard ready for burning. Rope clotheslines stretched across the yard, attached between an iron pole and the garage wall. The woman led them through the back gate and showed them four more garages, facing the rear street. "Six garages to rent brings in good money," she told Augustina.

Augustina looked across the street and saw that the entire block consisted of a vacant lot with a 3-story brick building at one corner.

"What's that?" asked Augustina, pointing to the building. Mrs. Soxmen explained that it had been a munitions factory during the War. It was empty now. They wouldn't be making munitions again, not after the War to end all wars was over. Augustina didn't understand the expression, but it didn't seem to be of importance.

Back inside the house, Mrs. Soxmen went to a drawer and took out a skeleton key so she could show Augustina the rooms upstairs. She opened a door off the living room and led them up the back staircase to a long central hallway on the second floor. Once upstairs, the key fit all the rooms. She showed them the house's one bathroom at the end of the hall, its door ajar. They looked inside at a claw-foot bathtub, and the toilet with a pull-chain attached to a wooden box. In the hall, four doors led to rooms that she rented out, three as sleeping rooms generally to men who worked in the daytime. Mrs. Soxmen explained that the fourth one -the front room - included a small kitchenette. Using her skeleton key, she unlocked one of the sleeping room doors and took them inside. All the rooms were furnished in a similar fashion with a bed including both a headboard and footboard, a large water pitcher set in a wash bowl on a commode, a drinking glass beside it, a dresser with a mirror, and a straight-backed chair.

Next, she took them in to see the kitchenette. When she again inserted her skeleton key to unlock the door and escort them inside, an irked woman tenant jumped up from a chair and stood facing them belligerently. Mrs. Soxmen quickly apologized for the intrusion, explaining that Augustina was here to see the house. Under the tenant's frown, the three took a quick look and left.

Once out in the hall, an embarrassed Mrs. Soxmen said, "I don't generally walk in like that. I didn't know she was home."

She took them down the front stairway to see her last rental, a two-room apartment in the front of the house. This time she knocked briskly on a door on the right-hand side of the hall. When there was no answer, she knocked again just to be sure. Then she unlocked the door, revealing a large living room that also served as a bedroom with heavy mahogany sliding double doors leading to a kitchen. The front room had flowered wallpaper with narrow border paper just below the 10-foot ceiling, as did most of the other rooms.

Augustina began counting the number of rooms on her fingers. Mrs. Soxmen said there were ten, adding that there was also an unfinished attic under the peaked roof. She and her husband were going back to Ohio where they grew up, so some of the furniture would stay. The property was 50 feet wide, 150 feet deep, and extended from Tracy Avenue to Virginia Avenue, the street the four garages faced.

It was a good location, Mrs. Soxmen said, just three houses from 13th street, that was mostly residential. The street to the north was 12th, busy with businessmen and streetcars and lots of stores she could walk to, including a grocery store and a drug store. The woman didn't mention the cabarets and speakeasies on the next block. These establishments abounded on downtown 12th Street in the early 1920's, with jazz and ragtime music and boot-legged whiskey. At night, painted women came out and wandered down the streets. Though Augustina was aware of their existence, it did not bother the pure, industrious, immigrant who generally walked down the street in the daytime. But even at night, if a decent-looking woman hurried along minding her own business, she was generally safe. That day, Augustina was unable to foresee any cause to be concerned over this neighborhood in the years to come.

In broken English, Augustina conceded that it was a nice house. "I'll be back to look at it again," she said. Sig repeated this in English – sans accent - to Mrs. Soxmen, who nodded.

Augustina and Sigmond left. Sigmond had been a remarkably well behaved boy while they were there, only fidgeting a little and whirling around to look at things they had passed, fascinated by what looked like 'cigars' hanging from what he called the 'cigar trees.' (Catalpa trees as we know them by their species' name.) He lagged behind in the backyard only once until Augustina had to tell him to come on.

As they started up the street, Augustina couldn't help noticing that the one-story house across the street on the corner of 13th had the neatest lawn on the block. An older couple was sitting in porch chairs, silently looking at them from across the street.

Next door to them, another couple sat in the porch swing of their two story home. A sign outside read: ROOM FOR RENT. The woman, who they would later get to know as Mrs. Needman, smiled at them. Augustina gave a little smile back.

Proceeding up the street toward 12th, they saw a man with a long black beard wearing the black hat and black suit of the Orthodox Jew, coming toward them. He never acknowledged that he saw them, but turned into a fenced yard where a small house was set far back on the property.

Farther on, two children about eight years old, were playing in front of a house. Augustina decided this looked like a good street to live on. She realized that it was a big risk to spend so much of the money Walter had left her, but she *really* liked that house.

To Augustina, 12th Street was busy and alive. Clanging streetcars came by to take her wherever she wanted to go. A drugstore and small grocery store stood on the corner a block from the house she wanted to buy. She was delighted with the accessibility of the other stores and small businesses. She could even walk downtown to Main Street, about eight blocks, where there were dime stores and department stores.

As they turned and started down Troost, an explosion suddenly rocked the street ahead of them. They saw a house erupt in flames that shot out from the windows and burst into the sky. Augustina and her son were terrified. Two women walking by were hit by flying debris. One fell unconscious to the ground. The other ran out of the way, screaming out loud in the highest pitch Augustina had ever heard. Sig leaped into action, running to the fallen woman, tugging at her arm, dragging her out of harm's way. Her friend came running back, screaming, "Thelma!, Thelma!" A policeman walking his beat came running from 12th Street.

Augustina rushed over and grabbed Sig by the hand, pulling him down the street, her heart pounding. Losing his father had been bad enough. She couldn't lose her boy, too! They stopped and stood at a safe distance watching people come rushing out of stores and houses. A fourteen-year-old grocery boy in a white apron ran out of the small grocery store on the corner of 13th Street. He joined the others milling around the two women hit by flying objects, listening with intent to what was going on.

As a fire truck came to an abrupt halt at the curb, several firemen jumped out to fight the blaze. The gas company was called to investigate whether a leaking gas main had caused the explosion.

The next day the Kansas City Star reported that it was a faulty gas main and Augustina fervently hoped there were no leaky gas mains under the house she wanted to buy.

As Walter's wife, Augustina had learned a lot of things, but nothing stood out more than what she called his greatest piece of advice when it came to money. The best thing an immigrant could do, Walter taught her, before going into a business deal, was to hire a good lawyer.

Augustina located an attorney named Ernst Lukas that she could communicate with in German and Polish, as well as the little English she knew.

She sought his advice on investing in the rooming house on Tracy Avenue close to downtown, three doors from the corner of 13th Street. Hesitantly, she told him about the money her husband had left her. This made Lukas the only person she had ever mentioned the money to since her arrival in Kansas City.

In Polish she told him, "I got to be sure how I invest it, so nobody can get it away from me." The attorney said he understood completely. "A woman alone has to watch out!" he said. But with six garages and six rooms to rent out, plus living quarters for herself and her boy, she told him she thought she could make a good living as owner of the house.

He nodded in agreement. A good rooming house should afford her the security she needed for a home for herself and her son. Real estate was a sound investment, one in which a person could not go wrong. If she paid the taxes on time, no one could take it away from her. Then if she ever decided to sell it, she should be able to get her money back and then some.

But Lukas did have a concern when he learned about the location of the house. He sat back in his chair and said, "I'd better tell you a few things about 12th Street." His account did not faze her. "Never mind that," she said, "I've seen 12th Street."

She said she liked to be near a business street, not stuck away in a residential area where there wouldn't be any close transportation making it hard for her to get around. She needed a place with streetcars nearby. She said the other day she saw some of the people who live on the street where the house was, and they looked like good people.

When he learned that she planned to pay cash for the house, he tried to explain that she could keep some of her money if she took out a mortgage and paid a little interest on it. Augustina said she never knew anybody who did business like that.

"My husband always paid cash!" She wasn't going to throw her money away on interest payments and worry about the mortgage.

"Maybe you'd better think it over," Lukas said.

"Well, I'm not going to pay anybody interest," she retorted.

The lawyer looked at her and saw she wasn't going to budge. After a moment, he said, "All right then. When you and the owner settle on a price, I'll go ahead and get the paperwork started."

When he was walking her to the door, he said as an afterthought, "The location might turn out to be a good one at that. The city has been talking about building a new highway through town, and it might go down 13th Street. If your property is three houses from the corner as you say, that land might become quite valuable." Augustina was pleased to hear it.

She left with one important request. Before she paid out her money, she wanted somebody to make sure there weren't any gas leaks under the house, like the one on Troost the other day. The lawyer knew all about it. He read it in the newspaper. She said, "Well, I don't want anything like that to happen to my house. I want to make sure it is safe to live in for many years, maybe even all my life."

Augustina and 11-year-old Sig moved into "the House" in 1920.

With her limited command of the English language, she seldom gave specific names to persons, places or things when she talked. The new home she was so proud of was "the House." Her son was "the Boy." His father was "him." Rather than trying to name an object, she frequently pointed to it and said "that," although without her ability to master the 'th' sound, it always came out, "dat." She was reluctant to reveal personal facts because she wasn't sure who it was safe to trust.

People found her last name, Kengerski, hard to pronounce. It was a constant issue when Americans tried to repeat it or spell it. Augustina decided to change it to a short name that even a simpleton could pronounce. Smith. Nobody questioned it, for it was a common practice in those days for people from the Old Country to shorten their names or take completely new ones when they came to America. Thus, she became 'Mrs. Smith.' She picked Ella for her first name.

In her new home, she was hard-working and happy. With a "rag," as she called her bandana, tied around her head to keep the dust off her hair, she hummed with contentment as she went about her work. Daily, she swept the worn carpet of the staircase leading to the second floor, and cleaned the upstairs sleeping rooms while the tenants were at work. She made beds, dusted, straightened up the rooms, and poured the water that the tenants used to wash in, out of the wash basins on the commodes into a bucket that she emptied in the bathroom. Then she rinsed out the wash basin and washed the drinking water glass, filled the pitchers with fresh water for drinking and washing again, and set them back on their commodes.

She scrubbed the linoleum floors of the house using a bucket and stick mop. She washed and stretched the sheets, sometimes asking Sig for help, then made the beds with the fresh linens.

The mailman, Floyd, became Augustina's friend.

In the summertime she tended the circle of hollyhocks and roses and other flowers and plants in her front yard, and hand-watered the lawn with a garden hose. GARAGE FOR RENT and ROOM FOR RENT signs were usually posted outside.

In the wintertime, she shoveled coal into the furnace, and before Sig was old enough to help, she shoveled all the snow off the front walk, driveway and sidewalk in front of the house. When necessary, with the help of her boy, she wielded a pipe wrench and made plumbing repairs.

The weather never went unnoticed by Augustina. She always had a comment to make about it. If it was really hot, very cold, extraordinarily rainy or other unusual or extreme climate, she would say, "I *never* saw anything like it!"

On pleasant days she would look up at the sky and smile and concede with satisfaction, "It's a nice day."

Augustina kept their own private rooms downstairs scrupulously clean, arranging things for convenience rather than for looks. She preferred to have much-used items in plain sight so she wouldn't have to go searching around when she needed them. For instance, she attached a ribbon to her pin cushion so she could tack it to the wall beside her dresser mirror where it was easy to find.

Many people didn't understand her ways. Sometimes she cut short a conversation by hurrying away to keep from exposing her limited command of the language. Her quick, sometimes brusque manner could startle those born in America who were used to more subtle interactions. She was proud of her hard work and the independence it gave her. No one could call her lazy, the way she thought of some Americans. She felt she had a right to an explosive temper when things got out of hand, and when she spoke her mind, this got the anger out of her system. Though her abrupt manner did stun some people, it helped her cool down and forget about what made her so mad in the first place.

One day, Sigmond brought home a little white puppy with black spots, one over his left eye, from a litter of puppies at Willard's house. He begged his mother to let him keep it.

"NO!" she said firmly.

But the Boy persisted, successfully persuading his mother to say yes. In her heart, Augustina, remembering her favorite pets in Poland, was certainly fond of dogs. They named Sig's new dog Buster. It turned out Augustina was actually very glad to have him because he was so alert, loving, and faithful, and had a sharp warning bark that made him a fine watchdog. When he was fully grown, someone once said of him that he was a medium-sized bulldog mixed with some kind of terrier, but whatever Buster was, he was a great companion and protector. Augustina, who felt lonely at times, found great solace in having such a loyal friend, who often tried to sit in her lap on those rare moments when she sat down, and lick her hands or face or whatever else he could reach.

Spontaneous parties began springing up in Augustina's quarters on Saturday nights after the Boy was asleep in an upstairs room and the door to the back stairway was closed.

Augustina was young and pretty and thwarted a procession of penniless would-be lovers. In those days, work was scarce for returning WWI veterans. She often suspected they were looking for a free meal-ticket, since she owned the house and they had few or no worldly goods.

On Saturday nights, roomers and other acquaintances came knocking on her door, some bringing a bottle of bootlegged whiskey. She got out her assortment of water glasses -- some were jelly glasses -- and they passed around the bottle asking, "One finger or two?"

Sometimes when they ran out of alcohol, if Augustina felt like it, she went down to the cellar and brought up a pitcher of her own home brew.

One of the regulars at her parties was Charlie, nicknamed 'Painter' because his trade was painting houses. He was tall, handsome and kind, a few years older than Augustina, but he drank too much. He was crazy about her and she liked him as well, but his heavy drinking foiled any chance he might have had of getting together with her.

A woman named June who roomed at the house for a while, never missed a party at Augustina's house unless she was too sick to come. June was about forty years old, had a whiskey voice, a broken nose, and once showed up with a black eye that an angry boyfriend had given her. June had no visible means of support, but she had a good soul. She loved to play records on Augustina's Victrola, which Augustina had bought at an auction house one day when she was out looking for used furniture and sealed trunks. This music was the highlight of June's life.

"With six garages, you ought to get yourself a car," one of the party goers told Augustina.

Augustina waved him away. "Cars are for men!" she said. The idea of her driving a car was ridiculous!

Usually there was much fun and laughter at the parties, but occasionally the evening ended with a fight exacerbated by the effects of bad bootlegged liquor. The participants often had severe hangovers and raw stomachs the following day, but they came back the next Saturday night to party all over again. Augustina knew at what point to stop her own drinking, having a strong sense of responsibility, and determined not to lose control of what took place in her house.

Sigmond hated the parties, the smell of liquor from the party room, the noise that kept him awake, the drinking, the arguing that sometimes got ugly and frightened him. But most of all he hated the men who came to the parties. They were always hanging around his mother. Augustina let the Boy sleep upstairs in a vacant room on Saturday nights, further from the noise of the party. A growing boy needed all the sleep he could get.

Sometimes Augustina told the party goers stories about some of her insensitive roomers. She told how the bathroom plumbing always had to be unstopped because of the stuff people disposed of in the toilet -- cans, dish towels, underwear, etc. She said she didn't know what she would do without her boy to help her. A man or two offered assistance but this usually came to naught because she had no telephone and she was never able to reach them when she needed them. Or there were strings attached to their friendly offers.

She also told of the "nasty-nice" renters who burned the lights all night long. She said that sometimes she got up and knocked on their doors and told them to turn them off. The ones who were the farthest behind on their rent were the most hateful, the most insolent, and left the biggest messes for her to clean up when she finally got them out owing several weeks' rent. The guests at the parties sympathized with her.

It was suggested to her on occasion, that maybe she ought to get rid of the headache and give up the place. Augustina was shocked. She loved her house and would never give it up for anything!

CHAPTER SEVEN

Then one afternoon an old touring car with suitcases, a tent and two fishing poles strapped to the sides, stopped in front of the house. The four adults inside craned their necks at the ROOM FOR RENT sign tacked up on the front porch post. A family from Thayer, a small town in Missouri, got out of the car. They were itinerant workers who followed the crops and didn't work any more than they had to. Art Pastor, the driver, hitched up his pants, gave a tug at the rim or his gray felt hat, opened the front gate, and walked up to the house. Art was a 25-year-old World War I veteran, handsome, blonde, single.

He was accompanied by his short, matronly, bow-legged mother, Drew Pastor, with intense blue eyes, roughed cheeks and dyed brown wavy hair.

Art's brother, Wade, also a WWI veteran, with bronze leathery sunbaked skin, a hand-rolled cigarette dangling from his thick lips, wearing a brown felt hat, sat in the back seat. Next to him was his wife Beulah, a thin woman with a long, pale face, pursed lips and accusing eyes that made her look as though she didn't approve of a thing that the people she was with were doing. She cradled a 6-month-old baby in her arms that she and Wade had recently adopted, swaddled in a faded blue blanket.

Art turned the manual doorbell on the front door and the grating ring was heard from inside the house. As he waited for someone to answer, he hitched up his pants again.

When pretty Augustina opened the door in her house-cleaning clothes, her hair bound up in an old scarf, she was embarrassed. The handsome blond man stared at her through the screen door.

She hastily straightened her head scarf and flushed. Pleased at what he saw, a broad smile crept over Art's face. He tipped his hat in greeting, then told her that he and his family were looking for rooms to rent. Augustina hesitated, looked them up and down, then told them to come in.

They wound up renting the kitchenette apartment upstairs and a small sleeping room down the hall from it. Not one of them had steady work, but in these lean times, that was not unusual. Augustina hoped they would pay their rent on time.

Augustina soon discovered that this "outfit," as she came to call them, worked very little and the two brothers drank as much as they could get their hands on. Their mother, Drew, was always happy to take a drink herself. Being veterans of WWI, her sons discovered that drinking was the only thing to get them through the horrors of the War.

Beulah was the only one of the bunch who did not drink. She treated the newly adopted baby, Earl, her joy in life, like a little prince. Even if she and Wade had nothing to eat themselves, they always managed to have enough money to buy the baby his milk. And if the rent was unpaid, well, that was the least of their worries.

Art was a happy-go-lucky charmer who played the guitar and sang folk songs. Even when in shirt sleeves, he generally wore his gray felt hat pushed back on his head. He perked up at once whenever the pretty young widow Augustina came into view, with her deep dark eyes, brisk, industrious house cleaning skills, and broken English. His eyes popped open even farther when he learned that she was the sole owner of this big, money making, house.

Art and Wade quickly joined the parties downstairs on Saturday nights. On some occasions Drew showed up. Charlie usually hung out near Augustina, as they had always done, enjoying each other's company. From the beginning, Art was jealous of Charlie's good looks and the attention he paid to

Augustina. Art wondered how he could somehow get rid of Charlie. Art was especially welcomed by the others because besides being so good-looking which the women loved, he brought his guitar, sang, and entertained them all with his musical talent. When he finished a song, he would wink at Augustina and if she were sitting close enough to him, he would chuck her under the chin. Augustina was flattered, but embarrassed. She came to recognize "Oh, How I Hate to Get Up in the Morning," and "Sorry I Made You Cry."

"I notice how *you* hate to get up in the morning," Augustina told him.

When he worked, Art was a truck driver. His jobs were usually short hauls. He spent the money as fast as he made it, mostly on booze. Between jobs, Art spent a lot of time out in the driveway with his head under the hood of his old touring car, with Wade helping. When Augustina questioned the way Art wasted his time, he said he was thinking about buying another old car, so he could repair it and sell it for a profit.

Wade, a painter and carpenter's helper, also worked part-time and like his brother, had no trouble spending his money as fast as he made it. His wife Beulah spent all of her time taking care of Earl.

Mother Drew made artificial flowers out of crepe paper. She sold them in cabarets along 12th St. in the evenings, or on the street in the daytime.

Art began campaigning to marry Augustina. She could see what he was leading up to. Realizing he was a repeat of Jan, she told him he was crazy! He didn't have a penny to his name, he was completely irresponsible, and he didn't think it was important to save up a little money or build up any kind of security to offer a wife. Since she owned a ten-room house and he owned nothing and had no ambition, it was obvious that he had everything to gain and nothing to lose if he married her. She, on the other hand, would almost certainly end up the loser.

But Art was a charmer and kept after her. One evening, after prodding her with a few beers, he caught her off guard. They were sitting alone on the front porch swing, when he started playing guitar and singing his best for her. Art had made pre-arrangements with Wade to ensure nobody disturbed them this evening.

That night, Art went to his room happy. He strummed quietly on his guitar, breaking out into the strains of "Summertime...and the livin' is easy."

The last time she used Walter's surname ~ Kengerski, was on the deed to the house, which she changed shortly thereafter to her new name Ella Smith. Art and his family only knew her as Smith, so nobody questioned it when she laboriously signed Ella (her nickname) Smith on the marriage license.

A great concern to Augustina was that she didn't want Art to lay claim to her house once they were married, and using a different name from the one the house was under was the only way she could think of to help fend off the possibility of being taken advantage of in the future.

Of course, she wisely consulted her lawyer, who told her it was the *person* that mattered, not the *name* she used, and she hoped Art didn't know that.

As a husband, Art turned out to be the way Augustina feared he would be. After they married, when he wasn't working at one of his temporary truck-driving jobs, or lying on his back out in the driveway tinkering with one of the broken-down jalopies that he and Wade bought and sold (and cheated a lot of people with), he was usually just plain lying around the house. Augustina was hard-pressed to get any money out of him, because his earnings went for booze or what Wade could whittle out of him to help pay the rent for his family and Drew. Augustina made it clear that the whole damn outfit wasn't going to live off of her, rent-free. Every time they fell behind, she said they better pay up or she would throw them all out. Wade and Art tried to kid her out of it, but she saw nothing funny about it and told them so!

Meanwhile she hurried about her daily tasks, sweeping floors, making beds for the roomers, tending to her irises, gladiolas, hollyhocks, and the other flowers the season offered. She continued to rent rooms to new tenants, yelling at Art to get off his rear end and pitch in to help her. When she finally got him to take a stab at repairing the plumbing, he botched things up so badly that she had to frantically turn to the Boy to come and help. Augustina kicked Art out of her bedroom and he had to go sleep on the floor in his mother's room for a week.

Art had a habit of taking money out of Augustina's pocketbook anytime he felt like it without asking her.

This included the times the ice man pulled up in front of the house with his horse and buggy. Art would hurry out and tell him how much ice they needed and what size bottle of booze he wanted. It might be 25 or 50 pounds or ice, a half-pint of whiskey or a whole pint, depending on what was in Augustina's pocketbook that day. Per Art's instructions, the ice man picked up his tongs and chopped off the block of ice, then threw a canvas tarp over it, deftly sliding the liquor bottle between the tarp and the ice, clamping the tongs on the already dripping ice block and hurrying it to the ice box inside the house. In the summer, he had to break into a run to keep the sun from melting the ice. He deposited the ice in Augustina's old brown wooden ice box and gave the bottle of whiskey to Art in exchange for Augustina's money. Often, more than half of the bottle was gone by the time Augustina, fuming, found out about it.

She was working hard at her housework one day when she began to feel woozy and sat down to rest. As she placed her hands on her stomach, she noticed it seemed larger than usual. "Oh, God, no, it couldn't be!" she thought. But the nausea she felt in the morning was the same as when she was carrying Sig. In the following weeks, she began to feel deathly sick in the morning and her stomach continued to grow. It was a shock and a tremendous worry, considering the fact that Art would be a terrible, undependable father. She put off telling him her suspicions as long as possible, but soon had to reveal the truth. Outwardly, she made it clear that she expected him to step up and pitch in, though knowing him all too well, inside she felt completely frightened and alone down to her bones.

Late one evening, Augustina with her expanding midsection, went upstairs to the bathroom. She noticed the light on under the hall door leading to Wade and Beulah's rooms. Since she had not heard any movement from their rooms in some time – at least a couple of hours - she knocked on the door to find out why the lights were on.

Receiving no answer, she went back downstairs to get her passkey and returned to unlock their door. Not only were the lights on, but all the jets on the gas plate they used for cooking were blazing full force. She concluded that they were using the gas for heat; irresponsibly leaving the apartment with the gas on, a terribly dangerous and selfishly wasteful thing to do. It meant nothing to that "Outfit," how hard it was for Augustina to find the money to pay for their inconsiderate behavior. If she couldn't pay, the electric company would shut off all the electricity to the entire house. Augustina decided she wasn't going to take it anymore! She extinguished all the gas jets and lights and stormed out.

Next morning, she bawled Wade out and demanded the rent they owed her. He said he didn't have it and since Art wasn't working either right now, he couldn't borrow the money from his brother. He tried to kid her along, saying it was all in the family now. Augustina shouted that she was "throwing them all out right now. That means you too, Art!"

She didn't know how she was going to get through the baby's birth alone, but she didn't think Art would be much help anyway.

Several months later she went into intense labor. Art had moved in with Wade and Beulah and their little toddler, Earl, into their new rooms over a store a few blocks away, with of course Drew. When her contractions began, one of her roomers ran to get Art. Returning with the neighbor, Art found her on the bed, crying out, holding her stomach with one hand, the other on her sweaty forehead.

Art sped off to the nearest doctor they knew of, a Dr. Council who recently moved up to Kansas City from the country. Then he went back to get his mother Drew. Dr. Council had a hard time understanding Augustina's broken English, so he called on Drew to translate. For the next six hours, Art nervously paced back and forth on the front porch, pausing only to hand-roll his cigarettes with trembling fingers, tobacco spilling out on the porch, then chain-smoking one after another.

Mother Drew clumsily did her best as she tried to help the doctor, sometimes misunderstanding his commands, boiling water and trying to follow his sharp orders. She certainly had all her differences with Augustina, but she knew that after all, this was *her* grandchild and she wouldn't walk out on them now. Drew sincerely wanted to help.

It was another difficult delivery for her, a 9-pound baby girl, a large child for a woman of Augustina's size to be carrying and delivering. This time her baby was breech. Dr. Council did the best he could with very little equipment to work with, using forceps as the only recourse. Piercing the baby's head and leaving an open wound inside the hairline above its forehead, he succeeded in pulling the child out of the birth canal and saving Augustina's life. The baby was born with the left side of her face twisted, her left eye squeezed shut.

Drew was heartsick. When Art came in and saw his wife and child, he recoiled at the bloody, twisted little face visible above the blanket. He took Augustina's hand and whispered with strained emotion, "It'll be better if she dies."

As weak as she was, Augustina managed to snatch her hand away.

"Go! Get out of here!" she screamed weakly. He stumbled out of the room with bowed head as Augustina looked down at her baby and cried. Mother Drew patted her daughter-in-law's hand and lost the battle of holding back her own tears. The two women sobbed together.

Weeping and distraught, finding herself in this extremely upsetting situation, giving up was never an option. Augustina defiantly named her baby Kristine, after "the prettiest girl she ever saw!" - the girl she had worked with at the chocolate factory in St. Joe. When she told Drew about Kristine, the older woman found it pitiful, what with how this poor little baby looked.

With Augustina in no condition to answer questions and with Dr. Council hard-pressed to understand anything she said in English, the doctor asked Drew for information he needed to fill out the birth certificate. Drew told the doctor to put the mother's maiden name as Augustina Smith, which she believed it to be. Also, she didn't like the name Kristine, so she told him to put down Mary as the first name and Kristine as the middle name, unbeknownst to Augustina, which she discovered at a later date.

Augustina let Art move back into the house with the agreement he would find work and pitch in. Drew stayed at the house as well and helped with the baby's care and did the cooking and made some of the beds in the sleeping rooms upstairs until Augustina got her strength back. Augustina appreciated Drew's support, since based on their past relationship, this was far from anything she would have expected from her mother-in-law. It was still a chore, however, to get Art to do anything useful.

Augustina faithfully bathed the baby's head wound and applied the salve the doctor advised her to use. She also massaged the muscles on the affected side of little Kristine's face, never giving up. At last, she began to see some results. After a few weeks, the baby's face started to re-shape itself and look normal. Hidden inside her hairline, however, was a deep scar that would never go away. But her baby girl turned out to be an adorable little thing, growing even more lovely as she got older, making Augustina a happy, proud mother.

As soon as she was able, Augustina was back making beds and sweeping floors, and Art began to do less and less to help. He never paid the doctor for Kristine's delivery. Augustina felt it was *his* duty to pay, not hers, and kept telling him so. Art protested unjustly that the doctor had botched the job by not delivering the baby properly. Art refused to acknowledge the fact that the doctor saved Augustina's life. Thus, the poor doctor's bill went unheeded and unpaid. (In later years, after Kristine had children of her own, she went looking for Dr. Council to pay him, but was only able to find his son, as the Doctor had passed away two years earlier. Kristine was so grateful to realize what wonderful people she and her mother had lived among, and made sure Dr. Council's son understood this.)

When winter came, a noisy one-ton coal truck hauling a ton of shiny black coal, backed up in the driveway. Augustina ran out and pointed to the basement window, then ran back in the house and down the cellar steps and opened the window from the inside so the coal man could dump the heavy load of coal into the basement. The coal tumbled out, its dust flying as it crashed to the ground. Augustina paid the coal man in cash from a handkerchief pinned inside her undergarment. Though she no longer kept her money pinned inside her clothing all the time, she did put it here on days she knew the coal man and milk man came so she could easily pay them.

Whenever the coal in the furnace turned to glowing red cinders, Art was usually nowhere to be found. Furious to think that he was probably out someplace having a good time instead of working as he should have been, Augustina had to go down to the basement and shovel more coal into the furnace herself.

Art and Wade saw a FOR SALE sign in the front window of a car parked on the street in front of a nearby house. Art bought the car, with its nearly bald tires, for next to nothing. Since he did not have enough money to buy the parts needed to repair it properly, he and Wade replaced two of the bald tires with a couple of used tires that were not much better, that he picked up cheap. Then, to lessen the bouncing and clattering of the car when it was driven, he put corks in the rear end of the car in place of shocks and springs, and sold it to the mailman Floyd, who had always been on good terms with Augustina. Floyd knew very little about cars, since like most people in the early 1920's, had never owned one, but trusted Art since he was Augustina's husband.

When the corks fell out of the back end of the car, Floyd, livid, returned to the house demanding to see Art. Art was nowhere to be found. The mailman pent his wrath on Augustina, who knew nothing about Art's devious transaction. She was stunned and furious. Not until a week later did he apologize. She was enraged and humiliated, ashamed to call Art her husband, and explained to Floyd that Art no longer lived here. When her baby girl began crying in the background, she yelled at the mailman that Art was the one he had to talk to! She slammed the door and broke into tears.

Picking up her baby, rocking her in her arms and soothing her with soft words, tears flowed out of her eyes. Then and there Augustina vowed she would get a divorce from Art. He was no good to her and now he brought her disgrace. He still had not paid the Doctor Council for Kristine's delivery and he probably never would. Any attempts he made to get work were too feeble to produce results. Industrious Augustina had prodded him to her wit's end, yet saw absolutely no change in her husband's behavior. Augustina swore to Art that she would turn him in to the police for selling that old pile of junk to the mailman if he did not leave and never come back. Protesting pitifully, Art packed his remaining few belongings and left, "swearing on a stack of bibles" that he would be back. Once again, he crowded in with his family in their new, cramped quarters where they already were behind on their rent.

One night, Art snuck in and kidnapped Kristine and took her home. Not until early the next morning did horrified Drew discover this. Kristine kept crying out for 'Mama'. Drew, appalled, insisted he return the baby immediately. Art was glad to get rid of the screaming kid.

"I was a fool to marry that guy," Augustina told Charlie a few weeks later at one of the impromptu Saturday night parties in her apartment downstairs.

Charlie sympathized with Augustina and jumped at the chance to make a pass at her, to no avail.

June was there playing the popular song on her phonograph, "Look for the Silver Lining" sung by Marion Harris, one of the first white jazz singers in America. She had a drink in her hand and slopped some of it over her arm, but didn't seem to notice as she happily hummed along.

Sig and Kristine were asleep in an upstairs spare bedroom, further from the noise of the party. This way she could check on the baby intermittently during the evening, and Sig could get some sleep.

Suddenly Art showed up, drunk. Seeing Augustina talking to good-looking Charlie whom he had always been jealous of, he grabbed her by the arm saying, "I got to talk to you." He began pulling her toward the kitchen. She reluctantly went with him since she didn't want to start an argument in front of the others who would probably tell everybody in town about it the next day. When Art slammed the door behind them, it shook Charlie up. He followed them to the door and stood outside, listening to make sure Art wasn't hurting Augustina.

In the kitchen, Art told Augustina he had news for her. "Me and the whole damn outfit, as you call them, are going to California in my touring car! We hear we can get work picking strawberries and plums near Sacramento. Then we might go down to Los Angeles. You and the kids are coming with us!"

"NO we are NOT!" she told him angrily.

When Art persisted, she demanded "Are you *crazy*? I'll bet you haven't even got a dime for gasoline!"

"We'll find work along the way."

Augustina told him she wasn't going to leave her house and her livelihood. And she absolutely wasn't going to take off with a bunch "who would crook anybody out of his money to keep from working!"

Art's voice rose angrily. "You are my wife and you are coming along!" He grabbed the little woman by the shoulders and shook her. Augustina cried out, "I am *not* going!"

Charlie, listening outside the door, rushed in to help her.

Art turned on him, accusing him of being too friendly with his wife.

"I'm not your wife anymore!" shouted Augustina, for in her mind she had already conceded that their divorce was imminent.

June heard the loud voices and came to the door in time to see Art yank open a cabinet drawer and pull out a butcher knife. June and Augustina screamed. June ran out the front door hollering, "Help! Police!" Sig woke up, ran down the hall, down the stairs, and into the kitchen in his undershirt and shorts, and saw Art chasing Charlie around the room trying to stab him with the butcher knife. Charlie kept ducking as he tried to get away, but the knife hit its mark a few times and his blood ran freely. Sig and his screaming mother were terrified. As the others crowded around the door to see what was going on, Charlie managed to wrestle the knife from Art and heave it to the other side of the room. A fist fight broke out between the two men, with each trying to retrieve the knife. The women guests, terrified at the bloody scene, screamed and ran out of the room covering their eyes. Art whirled and escaped out the back door, shoving June out of his way as she hovered in the darkness of the stairway, shaking, yet still eager to hear what was going on.

When Augustina realized that wide-eyed Sig was taking this all in, she ran to him and yelled for him to get back in bed. She gave him a push toward the back stairway, followed him, then slammed the door after him. Returning to the kitchen, she pulled open the drawers, one after the other, until she found some clean white rags, tearing them into smaller pieces that she could work with. She doused them in a pan of cold water and applied cold, wet compresses to Charlie's wounds in an attempt to stop the bleeding. A neighbor with a car helped dazed Charlie walk outside and drove him to the hospital. Augustina feared Charlie would be scarred for life.

Shaken, Augustina said, "That settles it!" She declared out loud for all to hear that she would see a lawyer and divorce Art before he killed somebody. His behavior tonight demonstrated not only was he a lousy father, but that he would not dare lay claim to any of her property!

The police found Art hiding outside behind the garages, hand cuffed him, and took him off to jail.

Charlie was badly cut, including a deep stab wound in his right arm which rendered it all but useless in the many weeks it took to heal. The right side of his face, below his eye, would be deeply scarred for life.

Following a short jail term, Art, claiming to be an innocent man simply trying to protect his wife and home, was released on bail which Drew and the family pooled together. She had to sell many artificial flowers to pay for part of the bail, and an old boyfriend of hers helped her out with the rest. Art somehow escaped town before Augustina could file further charges against him. Then he took off for California with his mother, brother Wade, Beulah and their little toddler, Earl.

CHAPTER EIGHT

Augustina called her new daughter "the little girl," and the little girl called Augustina "Mama." Augustina bought her son, twelve years older than his little sister, a good used bicycle and he proudly rode up and down the street and around the neighborhood of his Kansas City house – '1224 Tracy,' as it became known to them for years to come.

Each week, Augustina changed all the linens on the beds in the house, putting fresh sheets on top, and putting the old top sheets on the bottom. Then she put out a big washing, using a washboard and a bar of harsh laundry soap that chapped and reddened her hands, though she never thought much about this and never complained. In addition to the sheets from all the beds in the house, she washed all the towels, and all the personal laundry to keep herself and her children clean and tidy. She hung every piece out on the backyard clotheslines and took them all in when they were dry. It was a common sight to see the little woman carrying piles of fresh-smelling sheets and clothes into the house to iron and fold, which was another big job. Yet to Augustina, this was all just a normal part of her day. She called on Sig to help her stretch the curtains and sheets back into shape - she pulling on one end, he pulling on the other.

With intense manual labor on a day to day basis, coupled with raising two children alone, Augustina often found herself frustrated, resulting in harsh interactions with others. An emotional and scantily-educated woman like Augustina found it difficult to keep impatience and anger bottled up, knowing it would eat away at her insides. If she lashed out verbally at people, including her little girl, she did it really for herself to reinforce the strength and spirit she knew innately belonged to her, not realizing, nor feeling remorse, that it may have bothered anyone else.

There were many women more gracious to deal with, who would never throw you for a loop with a burst of temper, but there were very few who worked as hard, were as honest, or had as much integrity and loyalty as Augustina. She instilled integrity in Kristine, just as she had in the Boy, taught her children to "do unto others," be civil around other people, and always respect private and public property. Without saying it, and perhaps without even thinking it, she put forth the philosophy to her children and all those she came in contact with that if each person respected one another, it would contribute toward a safe, clean world for all who live in it.

She was never truly sick in her life. She always "doctored" herself and her children as taught by her Polish friend Ana back in St. Joseph so long ago. She bathed surface infections such as boils or a stye on the eye with hot water. The main thing she watched everyday was that the bowels in her family were continuously flowing. "You can't let the poisons sit in your body or you will get sick!" she said.

She blamed all other ills on food eaten in strange places such as restaurants (her God was her own home cooking, and one of her specialties was homemade soup), on tainted food bought at the grocery store, or the "crazy" weather.

Any hope of an education for herself now drifted away with her past. Where once she was eager and willing to fight for a chance to learn to read and write English, she now was too tired at the end of the day to put any thought into anything other than getting her sleep, let alone an education. This was the closest she ever came to giving up. Everything was for her children now. Besides, nobody she knew ever mentioned night schools in

Kansas City, and she was reluctant to go out looking for an adult school by herself, not even sure such a thing existed here.

In the wintertime, Augustina often closed off the kitchen, shutting the doors to the cold rooms of the rest of the house, and put the galvanized washtub she used for the laundry on the floor in front of the glowing iron stove she cooked on. She heated water in kettles and pans on the stove and filled the washtub about halfway, and when Kristine got past babyhood – about three or four years old, Augustina bathed her in the tub. This was Kristine's once-weekly bath. Kristine loved to splash around in the warm water while her mother gave her face, ears, and body a brisk scrubbing. When Augustina had to hurry because she had a dozen more things to get done before she could call it a night, sometimes Kristine cried out that her mother was too rough.

Drew never failed to send a Christmas box when Kristine was little. One December when Kristine was four years old and Sig was sixteen, a large cardboard box wrapped in thin wrapping paper that was half torn off, arrived from California addressed to Augustina. It contained several inexpensive Christmas gifts for Kristine and Sig from Grandma Drew and Art, the letter said, but Augustina was sure they were all from the Old Woman, as Augustina called her mother-in-law. Kristine was very excited. There were toys from the dime store, and a "cheap" dress, as Augustina put it, and thin red blown-glass Christmas tree ornaments wrapped in tissue paper. They all arrived broken.

"Awww," said Kristine, sorely disappointed about the broken ornaments, but very excited about the other presents that survived the trip. Augustina did not want to see her daughter won over by the once-yearly gifts. She knew Drew did the best she could, but she did not think it made up for the fact that Art never ever sent a penny for Kristine's support, and she was pretty sure he still had not paid Doctor Council for Kristine's delivery.

An accompanying letter from Drew told Augustina that Art and the rest of the family were still living with her. This did not surprise Augustina.

That summer, Augustina cut the little girl's hair short so she would be cooler, and it would be easier to keep neatly coiffed. In the late afternoons Kristine began to run out to the front gate with Buster at her heels, peering up the street, looking for a neighbor man who each day came home from work at that time. Augustina got a kick out of watching her. The man would turn onto their street from 12th Street, wearing a business suit, felt hat and a necktie, whistling a cheery tune and swinging his arms as he strode down the street. Pretending not to see him, Kristine would swing on her front gate waiting for him to go by across the street. When he came opposite her, he would call out cheerily,

"Hello, little boy!"

"I'm not a little boy!" Kristine would retort, pouting. But the next afternoon she would be waiting for him again to come whistling home, while once again pretending not to see him, and the same scene would play over again.

Solicitors who rang the front doorbell of Augustina's house in those days fared well if they had something to sell that had to do with "the little girl."

A door-to-door insurance salesman sold Augustina two small insurance policies to protect the little girl: one on Augustina's life and one on Kristine's. Security was something Augustina was willing to invest in, because she could well understand it. The insurance man rang her doorbell once a month to collect his premiums in person, and Augustina paid him in cash.

But one day when Kristine was around five years old, Augustina was in the back yard with her hair tied up in a "rag," her arms and hands smeared with mahogany paint. Kristine was watching her paint an old, marked up chest of drawers she had bought at an auction. Augustina heard the sound of the front doorbell grate through the house and hurried inside with Kristine following closely behind. She peeked through the lace curtain of the glass door that opened into the front hall. Through the open outside door, she saw the insurance man dressed in hat, suit and necktie standing on the porch with his briefcase.

Embarrassed to go to the door looking the way she did, she told Kristine, "Go and tell him I'm not home."

Little Kristine marched to the door and informed the insurance man: "Mama said to tell you she's not home!" Augustina threw her arms up in defeat.

Straightening the "rag" on her head, Augustina went to the door, admitting she was out in the back yard painting and he should wait. She went to fetch his money. By the sound of her Mama's voice, Kristine realized she had said something wrong, but wasn't sure exactly what it was. (Augustina then realized her daughter was too young to understand these subtle yet important behaviors around those who were 'one step away from a stranger.')

Another time when Sig was at school and Augustina was home with Kristine, an itinerant photographer came to the door with a bulky black box camera and a tripod. When he saw the little girl, he was delighted. He talked Augustina into letting him take her picture. It wasn't hard to do since she loved the idea of having a good photograph of Kristine, like the portrait she had of Walter that meant so much to her. Augustina allowed him to come in as far as the front hallway, where she told him to set up his equipment. He draped a black cloth over his camera and helped Augustina set up a cane back dining chair in the hallway.

Realizing it was rather plain, he asked Augustina if she had a fancier looking chair.

"Use this one!" she said firmly.

She didn't have a fancier looking chair and if he didn't like it, they just wouldn't take the picture. Augustina bought all her furniture from the auction house, and she never bought overstuffed furniture such as sofas or expensive armchairs. She thought it was unhealthy to bring such items into the house, since there was no telling who had used them before. Who knew if they were sick people or well people? Who knew for sure what had spilled on them? Augustina wasn't going to bring anything that could possibly be carrying disease into her house!

The excited little girl, her hair neatly combed, having grown out just above her shoulders by now, wearing her best dress, was ushered to the chair. She posed with a smile, looking into the camera lens, her head tilted just a little to one side following the directions called out to her. The nimble photographer disappeared under the black cloth and snapped her picture. Out of range of the camera, Augustina beamed proudly.

Kristine watched her mother powder her face with a powder puff, rouge her cheeks (Augustina, with her accent, called them "her chicks") preparatory to going downtown shopping. Downtown meant Main Street, eight blocks away. She paid either Mrs. Needman, or the twelve-year-old girl across the street named Rose, to look after Kristine until Mama got home. Augustina always brought back a small bag of candy for the little girl, and once in a while, a ten-cent present from the dime store. How eagerly Kristine ran to see what Mama brought her from downtown.

When Kristine was five years old and didn't know any better, she used to go upstairs to a room rented by a woman with a teenage daughter named Marion who sat in front of her vanity mirror and painstakingly put on her makeup. Marion used cold cream, powder, lipstick, various tubes and a compact, all of which fascinated Kristine. Every time she visited, Kristine would slyly slip one of these items into her pocket and take it back downstairs with her, where she hid it among her toys. She knew Mama would explode with anger if she found out what Kristine had done, but that didn't stop her. At first, the seventeen-year-old just thought she had misplaced her things, but finally she realized that nothing ever disappeared unless Kristine had been up there. Angrily she told her own mother, who confronted Augustina. Appalled, Augustina searched Kristine's room including the big cardboard box where Kristine kept her toys, and found all the creams, lipsticks, powder and rouges and suddenly burst into laughter. She hurried downstairs and got a dishpan and tossed all the loot in. She carried the pan back upstairs, still laughing. Worried Kristine followed her up. Augustina returned the items to their owner, and made Kristine apologize. The grumbling teenager found it hard to forgive her.

In the early 1920's, before television was invented, and not many people had radios, it was common for roomers to gather on the front porch, weather permitting. Sometimes Mr. and Mrs. Needman came over from across the street. They would all sit and tell stories either about things that happened to them, or that they had heard about. If Kristine was not out in the yard chasing fireflies that flickered in the darkness, she and Buster would join the adults on the porch. With her dog lying at her feet, Kristine sat on the swing beside her Mama listening to the conversation, the laughter, and the one man in particular who would raise his voice above the others because he thought he knew more than they did about the topic at hand. When she grew tired, she would lay her head in Mama's lap. While the voices droned on around her, she looked out at the street lamp on the corner with its yellow glow, or up at the brilliant stars and the glowing face of the man in the moon, until her eyelids grew so heavy she fell asleep. Augustina would smile down at her little girl and lift her up into her arms and carry her to bed, then go back downstairs and take her place again on the swing. Such evenings were happy and relaxing to Augustina. A fine ending to a long day of hard work.

There were no other children Kristine's age on the block. When Augustina was too busy cleaning the rooming house to be 'bothered' with the child, Kristine asked if she could go across the street and see Mrs. Needman. Augustina usually said yes, and took her out to the sidewalk, teaching her to look both ways before she stepped out into the street.

One day, after a horse-drawn wagon with a man calling out, "Rags! Old Rags and bottles!" had passed, Kristine, with Augustina's permission, ran across the street to where Mrs. Needman was sweeping the sidewalk. Buster followed her as he often did. Mrs. Needman greeted her cheerfully.

When the woman's work took her back inside the house, Kristine tagged along and begged her to sing that song about the dog that she always sang when she worked.

Mrs. Needman laughed and cheerfully began:

"Makes no difference if he is a hound,
Stop kicking my dog around, around,
Stop kicking my dog around!"

Kristine giggled with delight and imitated her, singing, "Stop kicking my dog around, around, stop kicking my dog around!" Mrs. Needman laughed and gave her a big hug, which meant the world to Kristine. Augustina would do anything in the world for her daughter, but hugging was definitely not something she did often.

One Saturday afternoon Augustina was boiling a pot of water on the stove, and stepped out to answer the call of a roomer. Kristine, who had been playing outside, ran in to bring mama a flower from the garden. As she was passing the stove, she caught the handle of a pot and scalding hot water poured on Augustina's left shoulder. Hearing the screams, Augustina rushed in, realized what had happened, grabbed her daughter and pulled her to the sink where she ran cold water over her, then chipped off a chunk of ice and held it on her burned shoulder. She called one of the roomers to help bring Kristine to the hospital, where she was treated and remained for three days to ensure no infection set in. For weeks after Kristine returned home, Augustina spread salve on the affected area to prevent infection, which eventually healed without incident, but would end up leaving a sizeable scar on the front of Kristine's left shoulder for life.

During the summer after Kristine finished kindergarten, Augustina went to a local bookstore and asked for a first-grade reader. Her speech and grammar were still at a beginner's level, but her accent was less pronounced now. She eventually managed to get the clerk to understand what she wanted.

Armed with the words she had picked up while trying to read the Kansas City Star, along with what she had learned from Sigmond's school books, she sat in a chair with her little girl and laboriously read to her from the first-grade reader. Augustina pointed at each word with her finger. She sounded out the words she didn't know, and got as much out of the lesson as Kristine. Though both very serious during their lessons, they always took the time to look at the pictures and laugh.

One memorable poem Augustina read to her little girl, pointing out the words, was AT THE SEASIDE by Robert Louis Stevenson:

When I was down beside the sea,
A wooden spade they gave to me,
To dig the sandy shore.
My holes were empty like a cup,
In every hole the sea came up,
Till it could come no more.

Kristine was delighted and fascinated with this new world of words. She wanted to see the word 'empty' again. It took Augustina a little time to find it. Kristine looked at it very carefully so she would remember it. Then one day in the two-story brick school house, she amazed her teacher by being the only child who could read the word 'empty.'

Augustina always stressed the importance of 'schooling' to the little girl, as she had to Sigmond. She explained that she must listen to what the teacher told her and she must grow up with a good education and get a good job working in an office. She didn't want Kristine to ever have red rough hands like hers from cleaning the house and washing dishes. Kristine must finish high school and be a smart girl.

Augustina sat at her treadle sewing machine making Kristine a loose fitting cotton school dress with the low waistline of the day, out of a cheerful flowered print fabric. Augustina always made sure that all of Kristine's dresses were bright and colorful, certainly not dull and dark like Augustina had to wear on her last day of school in Poland. It was a dreadful day she would always remember. Kristine was delighted with a new pocket Mama made her in the shape of a duck, which Augustina designed herself and applied with a hand-embroidered crisscross stitch to the dress.

Later when Kristine was a teenager, she told her mother how much she loved the duck pocket on that special dress. Augustina waved it aside saying, "Oh, that was nothing." But inside, it meant a great deal. Augustina was truly touched that Kristine had remembered the little pocket after all those years.

In the evenings, Augustina got the little girl ready for school the next day. Her clothes were laid out, her lunch made, or her 15 cents lunch money ready. Augustina made sure there were no missing buttons or snaps from her child's dress, nor any rips or missing belts.

It was winter in the early morning when Augustina washed the little girl with a pan of hot water and a washcloth beside the stove in the kitchen. She briskly scrubbed the little girl's face and ears until Kristine cried, "Ouch!"

"You can't go to school with dirty ears. Everybody will see them!" said Augustina.

While Augustina dried Kristine vigorously with a thin terry cloth towel, Kristine pouted and pulled her short hair down over her ears and scampered away as soon as she could.

Mornings, Augustina put an apron on the child so she could eat her breakfast without getting her dress dirty. When Kristine sat down at the round kitchen table, Augustina set a generous bowl of oatmeal before her while she made her a piece of toast over a louvered metal contraption which she set over the gas jet.

Augustina turned the toast over when she figured the first side was brown enough, and waited until the second side began to smoke. Then she quickly picked it off the toaster, juggling the hot bread in her hand, and dropped it on a saucer, scraped off the burnt part, and buttered it. Kristine was already heartily eating her oatmeal, which made Augustina happy.

That morning when Augustina walked her to school, Kristine wore her new dress and had one little hand in the duck pocket. Augustina laughed, pleased to see not only did the pocket look pretty, but it was useful too!

In 1927, when Sig turned 18, he moved out with his longtime buddy Willard, whom had stood by his side when the bully picked a fight with him several years back in grammar school. The two had remained close friends, and had the good fortune to find an apartment to share in a newly built area on the other side of town, or 'Out South' as Augustina called it.

One school day when Kristine was seven years old and in the third grade, Augustina looked out the kitchen window at the afternoon pouring rain, beating against the panes with a loud rapping, sound. Worried that Kristine would get soaking wet before she got home from school, she hurried to change her clothes and get her umbrella to go out and meet Kristine at school.

She walked as fast as she could the six blocks to the school house in the pouring rain, lowered her umbrella, shook off the rain, and stopped in the school doorway.

She followed singing voices to the third-grade classroom and stood shyly in the open doorway for the few minutes left until class was let out. Her eyes took in the room with the little tables and chairs, and a feeling of exhilaration and gratitude came over her. Kristine, who did not notice her mother, was sitting at her desk, attentively listening to the lesson.

A friend who lived a block away from Kristine and had been to her house, recognized Augustina, and whispered to another girl that that was Kristine's mother. The word was passed along until Kristine and the teacher heard. All eyes turned toward the doorway. Augustina smiled with pleased embarrassment.

When the school bell rang, the teacher, Mrs. Netherton, a tall, large-boned woman wearing black-framed glasses, introduced herself to Augustina. As Kristine stood by looking up at them, the teacher told her mother what a very smart girl her daughter was. She was especially good at reading.

Glancing up at her Mama, Kristine told the teacher, "Mama helps me."

Augustina was so tickled she could hardly stand it. On the way home, under the umbrella pelted by the rain, Augustina walked proudly as she held Kristine's hand, smiling to herself.

Augustina found a recipe book in a locked trunk she had bought at the auction house. Thumbing through it, she was pleased to find a section filled with interesting cake recipes. She began baking a different kind of cake every Sunday, and Kristine was thrilled.

She baked orange cake made with grated orange rind, black walnut cake which was Kristine's favorite, banana cake, chocolate cake, and coconut cake.

Kristine always looked forward to Sundays when she had her two pieces of cake-of-the-day – one after lunch and one after dinner. Usually Buster would be close to her feet, drooling hopefully, resting his head in her lap, waiting patiently for a chance to taste even a stray crumb of her cake. If Augustina saw this, she would protest, "Hey!, I didn't bake this for the dog!" Kristine would sneak a handful to Buster, then finish every last crumb on her plate herself. Later, before she went to bed, she would eagerly ask her mother, "What kind of cake are you going to bake next Sunday?" Augustina was pleased that she made her little girl so happy.

One afternoon, a gentle woman church solicitor came to Augustina's house inquiring if any children lived here. Augustina said she had an eight-year-old girl. The woman was canvassing the area to enroll children in the Baptist Church just a few blocks away. She explained they had a very nice Sunday School for the children. They took them on picnics in the summer time, and gave them little gifts at Christmas and Easter. The children learned bible stories, and they always enjoyed the singing. Augustina admitted that Kristine loved to sing herself, as well hear others sing and whistle.

"It might be nice for her to go," she said.

For the next three years, the little girl went to Sunday School. The first Sunday, Augustina took her by the hand and walked her the five blocks. Kristine was wearing her 'good' orange silk dress trimmed with cream-colored silk, that her Mama had made. It was her only 'good' dress, and she wore it proudly. Augustina took her into the church to find the class for eight-year-olds. A kindly woman took the little girl in tow, then smiled and asked Augustina, "Are you staying for church?"

Embarrassed once again of her lack of command of the English language, Augustina declined. Inquiring what time

Kristine's class would be out, she said she would be back to get her and hurried away.

For many Sundays thereafter, Kristine put on her orange silk dress and stood before the dresser mirror combing her chin-length naturally wavy hair. The ends flipped up on each side, often higher on one side than the other. Kristine fretted and stamped her feet as she tried unsuccessfully to comb the higher side down to match the lower side.

"Go on! You don't want to be late for Sunday School!" said Augustina. By that time, Kristine was walking to church by herself. True to the gentle woman solicitor's word, there were picnics in the summer time with sandwiches and potato salad, gifts of holiday wrapped candy for Christmas, and for Easter, Kristine ran home with a beautiful potted geranium which she gave to Mama.

The children sang songs every Sunday, and Kristine absolutely loved this part of going to church. An easel stood at the front of the Sunday School room with the words to the songs hand-printed in large black letters on a large white chart. Some of the letters were in handwriting, and Kristine couldn't always read them, so she a few of the words wrong, but she was the loudest singer there.

One day when Kristine was nine years old, Augustina was carrying groceries home from O'Connor's grocery store on the corner of 12th Street. She walked past a flat near the corner with a front apartment that had been empty for months. Now there were lace curtains in the front window and a girl about Kristine's age, with straight brown hair, wearing glasses, standing on the porch, looking curiously up and down the street.

Delighted to see a young child her daughter's age in the neighborhood, Augustina hurried home and urged Kristine to run on up and see if she could get acquainted. Kristine was as eager as her mother. She had waited for a long time for a friend her own age to move onto the block.

She flew out the door and hurried up the street to the flat, but by then, the girl was no longer outside. Kristine stood on the sidewalk looking up at the window, trying to see through the lace curtains. She finally gave up and reluctantly turned to go home. Just then the girl opened the front door and came out on the porch. Through her glasses, she stared down at Kristine. Kristine shuffled her feet and acted as though she just happened to be walking by. She tried to think of something to say.

The girl slowly walked down the steps and she and Kristine started smiling shyly at one another. The girl's name was Fern. She was ten years old, a year older than Kristine, and lived with her mother and stepfather, Smitty. It was summer and vacation time from school, so Kristine and Fern had plenty of free time and became the best of friends.

Fern was a nervous girl, easily frightened, but that didn't stop Kristine from becoming her friend.

Since most people didn't have cars then, including Augustina and Fern's folks, the two girls walked everywhere they went. They skated on the sidewalk near their houses. They went to the small brick neighborhood library and browsed among the children's books. Fern wasn't much interested in reading, but Kristine returned the books she had already checked out and read, and took out four more, the limit each child was allowed.

In exploring the library, the girls discovered that downstairs there was a small quiet museum where not many others were around. This gave them a chance to check out the private parts of a statue of a nude boy who was intently picking a thorn out of one of his feet. They stared and giggled, so they could see what a boy looked like down there, for Fern didn't have a brother and Sigmond certainly didn't display his private parts to Kristine.

They walked up to Eighth and Tracy to the Unity Church headquarters and browsed through back issues of colorful

Wisdom children's magazines, and under watchful eyes, each of them took home one or two, but never more than the maximum quantity of two that the Church permitted them to check out.

They walked to the Grove Park where they played on the swings, standing up and pumping as high as they could go, and swam in the public swimming pool.

They went to another park, the Paseo Park. There was a beautiful fountain, gushing water high into the air. Several people sat on surrounding benches, enjoying the fountain. They saw a man in a gray Fedora hat and worn suit sitting on one of the park benches. When Kristine and Fern walked by, the man spread his knees apart, revealing his pale private parts that shown through the opening of his unbuttoned pants. The startled girls ran as fast as they could, squeezing each other's hands as the adrenaline washed through their bodies. Then they stopped and hastily conferred with one another, then walked back, to make sure they saw what they thought they saw. The man again spread apart his knees, and the girls took another peek, then ran away as fast as they could go. They knew this wasn't right, but after they were at a safe distance, they held their hands over their mouths to stifle the laughter that brought tears to their eyes. They were afraid to mention this adventure to their parents, for fear they might not be allowed return to the park alone.

They walked down 13th Street and saw painted young women inside the houses pecking on the windows whenever a man would walk by. Some men stopped and looked up at the windows. One house had a half-dozen girls pecking and beckoning at the same time. Some of the men would pause and stand there making their selections, then walk boldly into the house. Kristine and Fern knew that these women were "street-walkers." They knew that some of the mothers of their own classmates at school were street-walkers. It was Depression time and with nowhere else to turn, several women in the neighborhood had turned to this profession to support themselves and their children. President Roosevelt had not yet initiated the Relief Program.

When Fern and Kristine, their eyes popping, saw them as they walked down 13th Street, they knew that at the ages of nine and ten, they were looking at something they were not supposed to see. Yet they could not resist their curiosity, as the women were all around them. When they got past the drama of the houses and the pecking, the young, innocent, naïve girls looked at each other and giggled.

Kristine never discussed this with Augustina. Her mother would have shouted angrily to learn that she was gawking at anything like that. There was no chance Augustina would ever move out of this neighborhood. This was where she had created her home, Kristine's school was close enough for her to walk to, and the high school she would go to in a few years was only three blocks away.

Augustina, whose strong scruples were much too sound to turn to anything like that, witnessed such scenes herself on her way to and from her daily errands, always hurrying on, minding her own business.

On one of her visits to Fern's house, Kristine was shocked to see several of her own tiny knick-knacks on the dresser in Fern's parents' bedroom. Fern's mother sauntered in to keep an eye on the girls and see what they were doing in the bedroom. Kristine knew that Fern slept in the living room and had no room of her own.

Realizing Fern must have stolen them when she was visiting, Kristine's eyes widened, her mouth dropped open and she stood there staring at the toys.

"Those are MY things!" exclaimed Kristine.

Fern's mother was just as shocked as Kristine was.

"Is that true?" Fern's mother demanded.

Fern began stammering as she looked for an excuse. Her angry mother quickly gathered up all the objects that Kristine pointed out and handed them back to her with trembling hands while sharply chastising her daughter. Fern was so stunned to be caught red-handed that she didn't let out a peep.

When the girls were alone again, Kristine angrily upbraided her friend. "You're not supposed to steal! I told you that. If you ever do that again I won't be your friend! Clutching her knickknacks, Kristine indignantly marched out of the house.

After that, afraid she would lose her best friend, Fern never stole anything from Kristine again. Kristine became very bossy with her to make sure Fern didn't get herself into trouble and steal from anybody else either.

(A few years later, when she was sixteen, Fern told Kristine that she didn't steal anymore, honest. She brought up the subject herself, and Kristine was surprised and very proud of her friend.)

When school started the September after they met, Kristine found out that Fern was put in a room with special, ungraded children who were slow learners. Kristine knew Fern was nervous and easily frightened, but Kristine certainly didn't see anything retarded about her. Although as they got older, it became apparent Fern was struggling to keep up with the other children in her grade.

When Kristine was a little older, Augustina took her daughter to go to see a movie every Sunday afternoon at The Central Theatre down on 15th Street, four blocks away. While it was only a neighborhood theatre, to the local people, especially during the Depression, it was a palace, with the most beautifully decorated ceiling with the fancy ceiling light they called a chandelier, and the burgundy velvet curtained stage, and the movie screen behind it -- very small by today's standards -- that carried them into the magical world of the movies. They saw such awesome offerings as "The Gorilla", a story about a trained gorilla who climbed up the sides of buildings and killed people at his master's command, and films with Janet Gaynor and Charles Farrell. Kristine found "The Man Who Played God" with George Arliss, an endless, tedious film during which the eleven-year-old shifted fretfully and squirmed in her seat. It didn't interest her in the least and she couldn't wait for it to be over, so she could go home. But she would never, ever think of getting up and walking out on a movie before she saw the whole picture, no matter how restless she was, nor would she ever interrupt her mother's enjoyment of the film.

So with Sunday School in the morning, a special Sunday dinner at noon with or without company, followed by one of Augustina's Sunday cakes for dessert, a movie in the afternoon, then more of Augustina's cake at suppertime, Sundays were superb.

When Kristine was twelve years old, she learned quite by accident that Fern's mother was a "street-walker." A man was passing by the flat one day when Kristine was on her way to the grocery store. She was still out of sight of the flat's window when she heard a pecking on the front window pane. She saw the man stop and look up at the window. When she came closer to the flat, she saw Fern's mother inside, pecking on the window, smiling at the man, beckoning for him to come inside the house. As he started in, Fern's mother saw Kristine. Woman and girl stared at one another, dazed, their eyes wide. Then Kristine blindly hurried on, wondering if she was at fault for coming along at that moment. Somehow, she never condemned Fern's mother for doing the best she knew how in order to feed her child and pay the rent. She never condemned Fern either, but always felt uncomfortable about going to their house from that day forward.

Soon afterward, another shock surfaced. She found out that Fern's stepfather, Smitty, was the one to solicit her mother. He was her mother's pimp.

Back on the home front, Charlie, with his scarred face, stopped by the house one afternoon while Augustina was preparing supper for Kristine and herself. Charlie had a brand new haircut that day, clipped very short.

"I told the barber to cut it short so it would last a long time," said Charlie, running his hand over the high-shingled hair on top of his head. He had been drinking and pulled a half-pint bottle out of his coat pocket that still had an inch or so of whiskey left in the bottom and took a drink while they talked.

"I don't have enough to ask you to stay for supper," said Augustina, referring to the food she was preparing, "but you better get yourself something to eat. You've had enough to drink, Charlie."

"I'm not hungry," said Charlie. He left to go by the bootlegger's on the way home and buy another bottle.

That was the last time Augustina or anyone else ever saw him alive. When they heard the news, in disbelief, they collectively pieced together and decided this is what must have happened to him:

Charlie stopped off at the bootlegger's as he said, for a bottle of booze was found in his coat pocket smashed "all to hell".

It must have been dark by the time he arrived at his rooming house with his bottle. Unsteadily, he climbed up the outside wooden staircase that led to a small porch with a door opening onto his second-floor room. He began searching in his pockets for his key, but couldn't find it.

Charlie must have cursed to himself and decided to get in by a window he had left open earlier, a few feet to the side of the porch. Climbing onto the porch railing, he reached out his hand to grab onto the window ledge. But Charlie lost his balance, falling to the ground and to his death.

Kristine went with Mama and June to the funeral, where the organ music played solemnly. Along with a few other of his friends, they filed by the coffin and saw Charlie lying in the satin lining, more dressed up than Augustina had ever seen him, looking peaceful and awesomely handsome, but very still and dead. June sobbed aloud and soaked her handkerchief with her tears, while Augustina eyes filled with her own tears, too choked up to speak. Kristine felt the same way and kept her handkerchief in her hand in case she could not control her own sadness.

A sister Charlie had mentioned on a few occasions at the happy parties at Augustina's house, showed up with her husband to take care of the arrangements. After ascertaining that none of the friends were present when the accident occurred, the somber couple kept to themselves.

Later, all the drinking buddies gathered at Augustina's house to comfort one another. They talked about what a good man Charlie was, and how he got all cut up that time trying to defend Augustina from Art. Augustina put Kristine to bed and then joined them.

"And he *just* got a haircut," she said emotionally. "He told me he wanted it to last a long time."

"It's gonna last a long time," said one of the men, and the others, in silent thought, nodded and mumbled in agreement.

Kristine could hear their trembling voices from her cot in the entrance room to their apartment where she was trying to sleep. The entrance way was her bedroom. No matter what came up in their lives and no matter what their surroundings were, Augustina kept Kristine feeling so secure that the world of grown-ups and the deep and complex effects of their tragedies was still beyond her comprehension.

By chance, the Boy stopped by the house the day after the funeral. He had gotten a job as an apprentice in a print shop. Since Augustina had no telephone, his visits were usually spontaneous, although for a period of time, he drove up from 'Out South' as she called it, every week or so in his shiny used Rio coupe, stopping by for a brief visit, and to see if his mother needed him to fix anything in the house. When Agustina needed help with the plumbing, Sigmond got himself all dirty working on the greasy broken pipes.

If Kristine was anywhere around, she came running to see her big brother. When Sig sat down, he sat near the front edge of the chair as though he wanted to be ready to jump up and leave as soon as he could get away. If Augustina didn't have a job for him, Sig never stayed long. He was anxious to get out of the old neighborhood as quickly as possible.

Augustina told him what happened to Charlie. Sig was terribly saddened, but said he was not that surprised. He said something was bound to happen to those bums who still came to the house from time to time to hang around and drink, despite the fact that Augustina's parties had ended long ago. Augustina was offended to hear her son speak so harshly about Charlie.

The boy wanted her to move away, to get out of that part of town – the old part, where houses and businesses were disintegrating before their very eyes. To Augustina, her son was not making sense. Moving away was out of the question. She couldn't leave her *home*! This is the center of her entire life. While she never went so far as to put her trust in people who drank, she said she would not fit in with the snooty crowd 'Out South.' This started an argument, then frustrated and angered Sig gave up and left.

Augustina felt blue. She decided to go get a drink to console herself because although she still had the company of Kristine, her only son - the Boy - had moved away and now with the untimely end of Charlie, she had lost a very good friend.

That evening she took Kristine and walked down to a small grocery store on Independence Avenue in the North End of town to buy a half-pint of whiskey from a man who owned a small grocery store and quietly sold bootlegged whiskey that he kept hidden behind a curtain leading to the back room. Shocking as it sounds now for Augustina to take a child along on such an errand to the notorious North End, she needed to do it for her own sanity.

Augustina always walked fast, and that night she walked too fast for her complaining little daughter.

"Come on!" Augustina said, holding her by the hand, pulling her along when she stumbled.

Kristine waited in the front part of the grocery store while Augustina and the aproned male proprietor went behind the curtain to the back room where Augustina made her purchase. Kristine looked around at the stacked canned goods and packages of food behind the counter. There was no self-service then. The clerk behind the counter had to gather up the customer's purchases and put them in paper bags. Kristine's eyes lit up when she spied several boxes of Cracker Jacks on the counter. Before they left, she talked Mama into buying her a box, so she could eat a handful as soon as she got home.

Augustina put Kristine to bed, then made herself a hot toddy. She heated water in a tea kettle on the gas stove, grateful that her new stove did not require her to fetch wood or coal to burn each time she wanted to heat something as simple as a little water.

She poured slightly more than a finger of whiskey into a jelly glass and put a spoon in it to keep the glass from breaking when she added the hot water. She set it down on the round kitchen table to cool. The light bulb hanging from the ceiling was only fifty watts, but in her grief, it seemed too bright. She went to the next room and opened a drawer and took out the letter she had received from her sister in Poland after the start of World War I. She turned on a lamp on the nightstand, and as its dim glow shone through the open doorway into the kitchen, she went back and pulled the thin chain which switched off the ceiling light bulb, then sat down with the letter in her hand, staring at it. So often she thought of her family over there and wondered if they had survived the war, and what they might be doing now. She wondered if she would ever see any of them again. Tears filled her eyes as she drank her hot toddy, feeling sorry for what happened to Charlie, sorry the Boy moved away, sorry for herself, and worrying about how she was going to provide for Kristine.

Augustina never got over the feeling that she was a stranger in America, and that most Americans didn't understand her. The truth was, they didn't, and the challenges of life proved to be a constant battle. Despite the underlying struggle, through her unwavering fortitude, persistence, and determination, she continued to do the best she knew how. After years of forging her own path and never giving up, she somehow always found a way.

One day, Augustina was busy sweeping down the hall stairway when the doorbell rang. A middle-aged woman in a dark felt hat, a long plain dark dress, fiery and hell-bent looking, missing a front tooth, stood in the doorway. She explained that she had heard a little girl lived here, and with a nod Augustina confirmed that she was her mother. The woman was seeking children to become members of the WCTU.

"The what?" asked Augustina. The woman could barely understand her.

"The WCTU. The Women's Christian Temperance Union."

Augustina had not any idea of what she was talking about. The woman launched into a loud explanation that it was a group of women vigorously opposed to drinking alcohol. The two women could barely understand one another, but the kind stranger finally got across that they wished to stamp out the evils of drink. And in order to do that, she said, they were going to have to start with the children.

Augustina stared at her apprehensively. In her broken English, she conceded that drink was bad, all right, if a person drank too much. The woman glared at her, not sure what she had said, then continued her ranting.

Kristine, who had been peeking from the lace curtain of the glass door leading to their quarters, cautiously opened the door and came out into the hall. At the sight of her, the woman's face brightened. She told Augustina that the WCTU had a Children's Chapter to teach youngsters never to drink. She wound up talking Augustina into agreeing to let Kristine attend a meeting of the Children's Chapter of the WCTU. The woman urged Kristine to bring any little friends she might have. Kristine brought Fern.

The two girls went to the WCTU meetings in a cold, bare room several times and listened to the fiery, dedicated women up on the platform at the front of the room preach against the evils of drink. The girls would exchange amused glances and try to keep straight faces. Both the girls' mothers, as well as Smitty, drank, and once in a while their mothers gave them a sip of liquor if they begged hard enough. Neither child thought there was anything wrong with that, but at the WCTU, they kept their mouths shut. They never mentioned their parents' habits either. But in the end, maybe the WCTU had something to do with the fact that with booze all around them, the girls grew up sober and were never enticed to follow the crowd, and never became dependent on alcohol.

If there was any painting or wallpapering to be done at the House and Augustina could not get hold of the Boy to help, she usually did it herself, attempting to persuade Kristine to give her a hand.

For wallpapering, Augustina put long boards together on tables pushed together, to make a large enough working surface for pasting the paper. She made paste out of flour and water and used a wide paint brush to do the pasting. She called Kristine in to come hold the pasted, folded wallpaper while she climbed up on a step ladder and reached down for it. She then stretched her arms up and held the wallpaper to the wall, unfolded it as she stuck it on and smoothed it out with a wide wallpaper brush. Restless and disinterested, Kristine grudgingly lent a hand only after Augustina yelled at her. It was a hard job for the small woman. Venting her anger helped her get through it.

Then there was the week's washing, a major job. After Augustina took in the last of her big week's washing from the clothesline in the back yard, Kristine, who often lapsed into a fit of pouting, was called in to hold one end of the sheet or curtain and help her mother tug on them to stretch them out, and help fold them, so Augustina could put them back on the beds and hang the curtains back on the rods. It was not uncommon for Kristine to be yelled at to help her mother finish the job. Although reluctant most of the time to help, Kristine understood the work was necessary to keep their home and a roof over their head. Over time, she realized that just because she didn't feel like doing the work, it wasn't worth being put out on the street.

To keep going, Augustina had to use little tricks that made her job as landlady a little easier. She only gave her tenant one clean sheet a week. This was not an original idea, as many hard-working land-ladies did this. She would wash the bottom sheet only, and put the top sheet on the bottom, then the freshly washed sheet on the top, and replace pillow case with a fresh one. If there were two people in a room and they paid a little more money, they got a bath towel and a possibly a hand towel.

Sometimes Augustina got so tired and frustrated with Kristine's attitude that she would sit down at the end of the day and pour herself a little jelly glass jar of one finger of whiskey, a little boiled water, sugar to her taste and a spoon to stir it with.

CHAPTER NINE

Augustina had no investments in the market during the Crash in October of 1929, but she, being a business owner, was drastically affected. By 1932, the Depression had undeniably hit home.

Worried Augustina had a serious discussion with the Boy the next time he came to the house. She told him that with so many vacancies, she could not meet her living expenses as well as pay taxes on the house. She had decided to rent out their living quarters, along with the rest of the house. She and Kristine would have to move out and find an inexpensive room someplace else.

The Boy agreed it was the smart thing to do. He had a few dollars saved from his job as an apprentice printer and would help her out if she needed it.

Augustina tacked a new sign on the front porch post: HOUSE FOR RENT - FURNISHED. It took a few months to rent her ten-room house, with one of the garages, to a large family that included four adults, two working and two looking for work, for fifty dollars a month. Then she rented three rooms for herself and daughter for fifteen dollars a month, a few blocks away so Kristine wouldn't have to change schools. Packing was a traumatic event for Augustina. She had spent a significant amount of Walter's inheritance to purchase the House and had hoped she would live here her entire life. Holding back her tears, she packed her and Kristine's belongings in boxes and old grips and moved out of the house she loved so much, the house that had been her security through good times and bad, for nearly ten years. In the new place, she turned two of the three rooms into sleeping rooms and rented them out to help pay for her own rent and food. She tried to rent out the four garages she had kept from the House, but never succeeded in renting them all out at once. This meant that whenever she had a prospective renter, she would rush back and forth to the House, taking care of this renter's paperwork, and the next time, rush back and forth to take care of that renter's paperwork. All the while keeping up on her current housework and current sublessors at the new place.

When Franklin Roosevelt was elected president, he repealed Prohibition. This meant in Missouri now, Augustina was legally able to buy a bottle of 3.2 beer, also known as near-beer, whenever she wanted to. Her sensibility always ensured that because her responsibilities to her daughter and to her tenants remained her number one priority, she never allowed her drinking to get out of control and interfere with what she knew came first.

Roosevelt's statement during his Inauguration Speech in 1933, "The only thing we have to fear is fear itself" became thereafter a well-known phrase. The new president initiated many programs to put the country back on its feet, one of them being the Emergency Banking Relief Act of 1933. This included food and a little money for families who had nowhere else to turn. Augustina would have died rather than ask for Relief. Even if she had wanted to apply, she still had the House on Tracy Street and as a property owner, was sure she was ineligible.

The family that rented the house could not find enough work to make their rent, so after a few months they moved out. They were decent people to talk to, but they left the house a mess and in need of many repairs which had to be taken care of before Augustina could get the House rented out again. Augustina, Sig, and sulky Kristine went in and papered and painted and Sig fixed the plumbing. The House stood vacant for several months before it was rented again. This time the tenants, a slovenly family, stopped paying the rent after they had lived there only two months. Augustina waited a few months to see if they would make an effort to pay up, and when they did not, she had to sue them out. To accomplish this, she hired her lawyer to serve legal papers demanding they pay up in thirty days or the sheriff would come and set their belongings out on the sidewalk. On the 29th day they moved out on their own, but not before kicking holes in the walls and stuffing tin cans down the toilet, stopping it up. Again, Sig was called on by Augustina to clear the pipes in preparation for the next round of tenants.

This turned into a vicious cycle and the House remained empty for longer and longer periods between tenants. With tears in her eyes, Augustina sat down and mulled this over. The House was close to fifty years old now and in great need of renovation for which Augustina did not have the money. She could not continue to ask Sig to keep pouring his own money into the place since he needed it to pay his own bills. She was obligated to hire her lawyer on a regular basis to serve papers to her irresponsible tenants who ended up getting three or four months' free rent before being forced to move. Augustina kept her head held high, assuming all the commitments of a responsible landlord, with mounting resentment toward the slipshod tenants who inevitably came out ahead every time.

The vibrant front yard of the House she had once been so proud of, with hollyhocks and roses and mint and climbing morning glories, dried up and turned brown. The exorbitant cost of repairs, taxes and lawyers came to more than she could ever hope to recuperate.

When the roofs of the house and garages began to leak so drastically that pans and buckets had to be placed on the floors, ready to catch the rain at all times, Augustina realized that the old house was too far gone for her to take care of any longer.

She talked it over with Sig, who tried to give her a little hope by reminding her that the city's plans to make 13th Street a highway were still under consideration, which meant a good price would be paid for the land, at least. Augustina contacted a wrecking company and met them at the House to discuss tearing it down. The man stood beside his wrecking company truck, placed his hand on his chin as he looked the House up and down, then, slowly nodding his head, offered to clear the lot and haul everything away for fifty dollars. Augustina, heartsick, reluctantly accepted his offer.

She went home, despondently opening her front door and walking into the front room. Kristine, immediately realizing something was terribly wrong, asked, "What's the matter?"

Augustina, too emotional to speak, shook her head, turned away and stared at the floor until she was finally able to tell her concerned daughter what happened. She added that she planned to keep the lot for speculation. With the House gone, the taxes would be lower and perhaps she could afford to pay them. She would try to hold onto the lot in case the plans for the highway ever came to pass. She clung desperately onto the hope that the city might still buy the lot.

She sent Kristine to bed and made herself a hot toddy and cried. Where were all the good-time party-goers who used to come to her parties and have a fine time every Saturday night? Nobody came to comfort her. Nobody cared, she guessed. Kristine heard the sobs from the other room and wanted to comfort her mother. She felt awful inside, but not knowing what to say, she said nothing.

During the next few years, still holding onto the empty lot on Tracy Street, Augustina and her daughter moved from place to place, sleeping in the same bed to save money.

Kristine was now attending high school. Augustina sometimes worked at a sewing job when she could get one, in a tailor shop or a curtain factory, but it was Depression time and jobs were hard to find. From time to time, she did housework, or helped in the kitchen of a boarding house. She took any kind of job that would pay their bills. It became increasingly more difficult for Augustina to pay the taxes on the lot where the House once proudly stood. The Boy paid the taxes for a few years, then decided it was money down the drain. When he stopped paying the taxes, and since Augustina did not have the money herself, they were forced to 'let the land go back to the city.'

Angry over losing her inheritance from Walter on the House, she recalled her lawyer's endorsement of the purchase. "You can't listen to anybody! Even the people you pay to give you the right advice!" she cried to whoever was around to listen. Then she blamed President Hoover for her hardship, as did many Americans, for the U.S.'s economical crash leading to the Great Depression and the loss of so many jobs and homes. Later when Roosevelt was elected, she blamed *him* for the nation's hard times.

Those days, Augustina worried non-stop. She often lay awake in bed with an aching heart, worrying about how she and Kristine could keep on going. Still too proud to accept the Relief offered by Roosevelt's administration, she used her own resourcefulness throughout the Depression to make sure all the necessities were taken care of for her daughter and herself, squeezing her pennies, holding down a job wherever she could, frugally dipping into the meager savings that remained, and keeping her commitment of never dreaming of being without a bank account.

She would rent a flat or small house. She and Kristine would live in two of the rooms, making one the kitchen and one the bedroom. The two or three extra rooms she furnished and rented out as sleeping rooms to pay rent for herself and Kristine and feed them both. She thought it was terrible that neighbors born right here in America would go on Relief. She thought that if they tried as hard as she did, they could make it on their own, too!

And, of course, there were women who resorted to a different way to pay their bills and support their children. The painted women on the streets and in whorehouses pecked on the front windows to attract the attention of the men passing by, attempting to lure them inside.

When Kristine protested that they should move to a *modern* apartment with steam heat, Augustina retorted, "We have to go where my pocketbook takes us."

These days parties were out of the question. Augustina was much too busy worrying about survival to even think of having parties. Since she moved out of The House where the carefree parties were held, June and the other party-goers had scattered in a scramble to provide for their own existence. Everybody she ran into mourned the fact that she lost the House. The fun and laughter were over. One time she ran into tipsy June who asked if she could borrow money to buy a bottle. Augustina did not accommodate her. None of the old crowd was in any position to help Augustina now that she and her daughter desperately needed them. In time, they all dribbled out of her life.

The Boy occasionally came to visit, whenever he felt his mother had no one else to turn to, but always sat on the front edge of a straight chair, ready at the first chance to hop up and go back to the other side of town that he now called home.

Kristine found out that Mr. and Mrs. Needman had moved away from the old block and rented a smaller house. She managed to stop by and see them a time or two.

The new people that Augustina met found it hard to understand her abrupt, broken English. They were startled by her sharp, outspoken manner. Americans did not understand her nature at all. They could not know the honest, loyal person she was because it was too difficult to get close enough to discover her huge heart and abounding kindness lying just beneath her rough surface.

Augustina never took on the American habit of borrowing on credit. She saved up her money so she could pay cash for everything she bought. If she didn't have the cash, she chose to do without it. She was always conscientious of rules and laws and the necessity to follow them for the good of all. She referred to the politicians and the government as the "Higher-Up" and "They."

Even when Augustina experienced heartache and did not know where to turn for solace, she knew she had to keep on going in order to support her daughter at least until she graduated from high school.

When she was lucky enough to find a job, she went to work six days a week, the norm for a work week back then, without overtime. If she got sick, which was rare, she doctored herself at home with a "physic" and Vicks' Vaporub, or whatever it took to ensure she got up the next morning to go to work and not miss a day's pay. Kristine remembered one time in particular when her mother had a very bad cold, a red, stuffy nose, and was so weak she was barely intelligible when she talked. She went to bed early in the evening, so she could get up at 5 a.m. the next morning and go to work. From the way she felt and acted when she went to sleep, Kristine truly thought her mother would never make it through the night. But Augustina awoke feeling remarkably better, and she determinedly, without *question*, got up and went to work, without any interruption in bringing in her day's pay.

When Augustina had anything she wanted to write, she called on Kristine to help her spell out the words.

"I want to scratch a few lines to Drew," she said one day after receiving a letter from Kristine's grandmother. Drew's letter contained a picture of Art in Egyptian costume for another role as Extra in a movie. Kristine gaped at the picture. "He's still in the movies!" she said in awe. His work was intermittent, but Kristine found it very glamorous.

Augustina didn't share her daughter's admiration for Art. She figured he was still drinking up his money the way he did when he lived in Kansas City. She knew for certain that he never sent a penny to help out with raising Kristine. The Boy spent more money on his sister than her father ever did.

Anxious to meet her bills on time, Augustina sometimes became very irritated, and Kristine had to take the brunt of her temper. The girl had grown up to be a stubborn, rebellious teenager, confident that she knew everything there was to know, and that her mother from the Old Country would never understand how a young American girl should dress and act!

One day on her way home from school, Kristine was walking past a flat when someone called her name. She turned and was delighted to see Fern! After they moved away from Tracy Avenue and Fern went to another school, they had lost track of each other. They were so happy to see one another again. Fern invited her inside where Kristine saw Fern's mother, Violet, still very attractive and wearing plenty of makeup with her eyebrows drawn in a thin line above her large brown heavily eye-lined eyes.

The two girls got to talking and laughing and eating cookies that Violet brought served to them. They forgot all about the time.

Meanwhile, at home, Augustina was frantic with worry over why her daughter was not home. They had no telephone; therefore, she had no way of calling anyone to ask if they had seen Kristine. It wasn't until sometime later that Kristine came sauntering in with no idea in the world of the misery she had caused her mother. Augustina shouted at her and angrily bawled her out, pushing her against the wall. The girl shouted back, and a shoving match ensued. Kristine finally backed down and ran to her bed crying, the bed they would be sleeping in together, as angry as her mother. Caught up in her own defense, she had no idea what she had put her mother through. But she was so mad, she had no regrets.

At home in the evenings, Augustina washed the dishes, mended stockings, hemmed Kristine's dresses, got out the ironing board and did the majority of the ironing once a week, though sometimes there was touch-up work or something unexpected to iron in between.

Kristine's dresses were few, but they were immaculate when she left the house, and her hair was always neatly combed, soft and shiny from being freshly washed. Augustina continued to make her wear each dress two days in a row to save herself half the washing and ironing. However, she always ironed the dress for the second day, and was actually glad to do it so Kristine would look proper and fastidious, even though she had to heat up the iron on the stove over and over to keep it hot until the dress was pressed in its entirety. If Augustina inadvertently missed one wrinkle, Kristine screamed in protest until exasperated Augustina put it back on the ironing board, put a damp cloth over it, heated up the stove once more, and ironed out the wrinkle.

The girl was usually dreamy, and hardly any help around the house. This was partly due to the fact that Augustina never wanted her daughter to help with the dishes or housework when she was younger and was actually *willing* to help. Augustina insisted her daughter keep her hands out of the dishpan water, so she wouldn't get rough, red hands the way she herself did from her daily use of the harsh household soaps. Kristine, *her* child, was very special, and she wanted to make sure she grew up to be a special young lady. "You just do your homework and when you graduate you can get yourself a good job in an office," she always told her. "You don't want to be a scrub-woman!" If I could have learned to spell and write better, I wouldn't be in this mess now. I was always held down because I didn't have any schooling."

Kristine did her homework faithfully, though not always happily when she found it too difficult. She was one of the brightest students in her class.

In the evening, when her homework was finished, she sometimes asked her Mama to tell her more about life in the Old Country.

She was fascinated that in Augustina's school, the lessons were taught in three languages, Russian, Polish and German - two hours of each. She wanted to hear her mother rattle off some of these languages.

Augustina laughed. She was pleased, but Kristine felt there was something mysterious about the way her mother shared the information. It was so long since Augustina had spoken any of those languages that she had nearly forgotten them. She didn't have any reason to remember them because she had no one to talk to, and she always wanted to be American anyway.

Kristine picked up a pencil and her school tablet and urged her mother to tell her how to say "girl" in all three languages.

Russian:	девушка
Polish:	dziewczyna
German:	Mädchen

After her mother told her, she wanted to know how to say boy, school, dog, cat, and many more words and phrases. She made a chart with a list of the words in all three languages. Augustina could not help her with the spelling, so Kristine spelled the words phonetically as best she could, listening to Augustina's rolled R's and other unfamiliar pronunciations.

When Kristine insisted on hearing even more words, Augustina stumbled, trying to remember them all from so long ago. She told her daughter that she lived in Poland out in the country and that her family spoke German at home. Kristine wanted to know what town she was born in. Augustina pronounced it 'Sedovna' but didn't know how to spell it. It was near Warsaw.

Kristine's teacher, Mrs. Nevins, always kept her ears open to learn as much as she could about her students. She found out that Kristine's German mother from the Old Country was struggling to support her daughter and making ends meet. One day she asked Kristine to stay after school. Surprised, Kristine wondered if she had done something wrong.

After their talk, Kristine came home with the news that her teacher's aunt was ill in bed. Mrs. Nevins took care of her at night, but she needed someone to take care of her in the daytime, cook and do the housework for several weeks until she was better. Would Kristine's mother be interested in taking the job?

Augustina was honored that a *teacher* would single her out for the job. When they met, Augustina was almost in awe of her. Mrs. Nevins said she was impressed with how smart Kristine was, and how neat and clean she always looked when she came to school. She would be happy to have her mother look after her aunt. The wages were small but a godsend to grateful Augustina.

When something came up for Augustina to write down in her new job as caregiver, she was embarrassed and explained her spelling wasn't so good. Mrs. Nevins understood and wound up giving her The Morrison Speller and Workbook, for grades 2 through 8, published in 1930. Blank pages were provided in the back of the book for the student to write both common as well as difficult words that might make the learning easier.

Knowing how much her mother wanted to improve her English, Kristine promised to help her in spelling and grammar. Augustina could hardly wait to get started. (In the years ahead, she kept the Morrison Workbook handy, and often searched through it for words she didn't know how to spell, or tricky words that she often confused such as 'suggest' and 'succeed.' She ended up filling in all the pages. She never tried to use an American dictionary because of the tricky way English words do not sound the way they are spelled, making searching for a word nearly impossible for her.

By the light of a 60-watt bulb hanging from the ceiling from a bare wire, Kristine, sometimes impatiently, guided her mother in writing exercises. She examined pages of handwriting which Augustina had tediously copied from text in a psychology book she picked out at the library. When she had lots of uninterrupted time, her handwriting was beautiful, flowing, and legible to everyone.

Kristine praised her mother's careful writing. The letters were so even, the slant was excellent. Augustina was very pleased, but modest about it. She laughed that she didn't understand the meaning of what she was writing, but she liked to write the words anyway. She knew she was under great tutorship, as Kristine's Freshman English teacher spoke highly of her daughter's exemplary writing skills, complimenting her in particular on her recent term notebook.

Kristine corrected her mother's double-negative grammar, helped her learn to tone down her rolling R's, and tried desperately to get her to say the 'TH' sound, instead of 'D' or 'T'. That was the most difficult sound of all for Augustina, since in all the other languages she had ever spoken, there was no 'TH' sound. She would have to train her tongue to move to the front of her mouth beneath her front teeth in order to master this sound, something that she was never quite able to accomplish.

Kristine brought her mother books in Russian and German from the library's foreign language section. Although she loved these books – it brought familiarity to her in their origins, and, she had a love in general for reading - she could hardly understand their meaning since they were adult books whose words were much more difficult than those she had learned to read in first grade in Poland. Kristine encouraged her to go to the library by herself.

Augustina loved the library. With Kristine's urging, she began going often and took out one or two books at a time, always Russian, Polish or German, the tongues of which she had once spoken daily, yet now remembered very little.

Augustina, bearing all the responsibility of taking care of them both, was thrilled to be on the receiving end of learning, but was very worried about Kristine's deep interest and serious attitude toward becoming a writer herself. The girl loved to write and thought she would get rich from her career as a writer, thinking she would never have to work or wash dishes again.

Augustina was aghast. "Get that out of your head!" she screamed at her daughter. She feared that Kristine was acting just like her father, Art, always looking for ways to avoid work. She insisted that Kristine get some sense in her head, so she could get a job in an office where she could make a good living.

Augustina found a small two-story house on Forest Avenue with four rooms she could rent out to pay their monthly expenses and meals. She kept two rooms for themselves, including a large, cluttered but clean housekeeping room with an alcove for cooking, making the combination a kitchenette. There was a small wood-burning stove in the center of the big room for heat, and a double bed in one corner which Augustina and her daughter shared. The room was originally a living room and had no closet, so Augustina fashioned a makeshift one with a pair of second-hand floor-length velvet draperies along one wall attached with a heavy cord strung through the top. To get to their clothes, she and Kristine had to pull back one of the panels.

A modern interior decorator would throw up their hands in horror to think of living in such a place. But Augustina kept the faded rug swept with a broom, and the alcove's linoleum floor scrubbed immaculately.

As always, she made sure that Kristine had enough to eat and looked "decent" when she went to school. If they didn't have enough for two normal servings at a meal, Augustina would put the biggest amount on Kristine's plate. At first the girl was too young to notice this, but as she grew older she pointed it out. Augustina assured her it was okay, and told her to go ahead, eat what had been given to her. Kristine couldn't help but be touched by this.

But often Kristine demonstrated stubborn and rebellious behavior, and bitterly complained about her mother's table manners. Augustina regularly stood up when she ate and hurried her own meal so she could serve Kristine and make sure she ate everything on her plate, because Augustina wouldn't think of ever throwing any food away. And she knew nothing at all about which fork or spoon or knife you were supposed to use when you were in company. They only owned a few mismatched eating utensils which they had to use over and over throughout the day, after they'd been hand washed, dried, and put back in the drawer.

"I wouldn't know *what* to use if I was ever invited to a nice place!" Kristine whined.

She often complained about the nourishing food Augustina served her, instead of "making a meal out of gooey cinnamon rolls, sugared cocoa and hot dogs, the way everybody else did," Kristine exaggerated.

Of breakfast, Kristine would say, "Oh, do I *have* to have eggs again?"

The hot, nourishing homemade soups and stews Augustina served for dinner, their midday meal, and supper, at around 5 p.m., were no longer good enough for Kristine. She picked even the tiniest of cooked tomato bits out of Augustina's delicious homemade dishes, infuriating her mother.

"You just slap everything down on the table!" Kristine would complain. "What if I need a napkin?"

"Get up and get it yourself!" Augustina would retort.

When her mother cooked vegetables, she always served some of the vegetable juice with them, either on the plate or by itself in a small bowl.

One day, Kristine was invited to stay for supper at a girlfriend's house. Her eyes widened in disbelief when the mother poured all the juice from the cooked peeled potatoes down the kitchen sink before serving them. They put out one fork and one spoon for each of them at their place at the table. Kristine nearly broke out into a nervous sweat as she watched to see which one they ate with, then she did the same. Anxious to appear as though she was an experienced and well-mannered table guest, she survived her first ordeal of its kind, she was greatly relieved when the evening was finally over.

In time, Kristine grew impatient in her role as her mother's tutor in the English language. She had classmates and clothes and boys, or rather, boys, classmates and clothes – on her mind, and Augustina wasn't grasping the reading and writing fast enough for Kristine. Her mother often forgot the spelling and grammar and continued to make the same mistakes. Kristine told her Mama she was dumb! She demanded to know why she couldn't remember anything from one day to the next!

Augustina angrily defended herself. Her mind was not as free as Kristine's. She was tired from working all day and she had many worries on her mind. She had to figure out how to be able to buy food and keep a roof over their heads. Kristine's tutoring became sporadic, accomplishing less and less, often ending in a quarrel, until finally it was discontinued altogether.

Bing Crosby was a big, popular movie star at the time. He was both a singer and comedian and Kristine became an ardent fan. She would go to a used magazine store on Troost Avenue and buy back-issue magazines and read publicity department generated stories of her hero and cut out his pictures. Whenever she got two of the same picture, she shared it with a girl in her sewing class named Rose.

She believed every word in the stories she read, and told her mother, "I'm going to be a writer when I get out of school so I won't have to work."

Again, Augustina demanded she get this notion out of her head if she thought being a writer meant she was allowed to be lazy. Kristine's father didn't like to work either and that's probably why he became an actor. Kristine had better learn her typing and shorthand and get herself a sensible job so she could pay her bills instead of looking for ways to be lazy. Kristine pouted and said she didn't care what her mother thought, that's what she wanted to do! Remembering how her Freshman English

Teacher had praised her writing, Kristine wanted to become a writer more than ever.

A few of the girls Kristine knew in school already had boyfriends with whom they went out on dates. Of course, they were a year or two or three older than she was. Kristine complained to Augustina that she wouldn't dare bring anybody to the cluttered kitchenette they had to live in with the bed in the corner and the wood-burning stove in the middle of the room. "Everybody else lives in a nice apartment with steam heat!" she shouted.

"Yeah, and a lot of them are on Relief!" Augustina shot back. "I make my own way!"

Some of Kristine's school-girl friends wore blood-red lipstick. And some plucked their eyebrows in thin lines the way Fern's mother did, and one even plucked out all her eyebrows and drew thin high arches in black pencil over her eyes. Some of the girls whispered that she was "fast."

Kristine did not want to pluck her eyebrows because she tried it once and it hurt too much. What she really wanted was to wear lipstick. When she told her mother that, Augustina hit the ceiling. She was not going to allow her thirteen year old to go around with painted lips. Kristine shouted at her mother that she was old-fashioned. She said the only thing Augustina understood was the Old Country, and Kristine certainly wasn't going to go around looking like she came from there!

Augustina was so distraught that she went to a public telephone and called the Boy, asking him to come and help her make Kristine stop putting "that stuff!" on her face. She was downtown on Main Street shopping when Sig came by the house and Kristine opened the door. Sig had a grave talk with her. He told her she shouldn't wear face powder because it was bad for such a young girls' complexion and made her look dumb.

Startled, Kristine glumly looked back at him. There was obviously miscommunication here. He thought "that stuff" their mother was talking about was face powder, and Kristine kept her mouth shut. If Sig saw face powder as this bad, imagine how he would have felt about lipstick? If Sig knew she wanted to wear lipstick, he would have really let her have it. Sullenly, she promised her older brother she wouldn't wear any face powder. He got tired of waiting around for Augustina to come home, and was gone by the time she got back. Kristine told her mother he had come by and that she promised him not to wear makeup any more. She ran out of the room when Augustina tried to question her further.

After that, Kristine took change out of her lunch money and bought herself a tube of blood red lipstick at the dime store. She waited until she got to school to put it on, and it made her feel smart and pretty and in with the crowd.

Kristine had another bitter complaint: She didn't have enough clothes. Augustina shouted that she worked hard to keep her clothed, clean, fed, and acting decent. "When you finish high school and get a job, you can buy your own clothes!"

Kristine considered her mother impossible! In her mind, if Augustina chose to, she could give her everything she wanted. She boasted about the wisdom of her school friends and *their* parents, who knew what Americans were supposed to act like and dress like! Augustina was at once on her guard. More enemies, it seemed, had surfaced for her to contend with. She never really felt like an American, and now these people were trying to take her daughter's loyalty away from her. Augustina and Kristine started pushing and shoving each other as they argued emotionally. They almost came to blows before Kristine turned and ran outside, slamming the door behind her.

Sigmond came by again soon afterward to find out if Kristine had kept her word about the face powder. "Yes, and she hasn't tried to wear any of the bloody-looking lipstick either," said Augustina.

Sig brought his lovely girlfriend, Dorothy Wyeth, with him. She was a poised, composed, graceful woman, with perfect posture, kind eyes and a beautiful smile. Kristine was in awe of her because she was so pretty, her manners were refined, her clothes were well-fitting and immaculate, and best of all, she was cheerful and kind and interested in Kristine.

Kristine felt honored when Dorothy passed on clothes to her, fresh out of the cleaners. They looked brand new and were more expensive than her mother could have ever bought her. Dorothy's first second-hand gifts were a soft cotton, loose knit orange short-sleeved sweater with a beautiful brown wool skirt, all freshly cleaned, folded and presented as though they just came from the department store.

For Kristine, it was very important to look cool and please her classmates, and it seemed to her she always had to fight her mother in order to do this. When the next school semester started, Sig gave Dorothy money to take Kristine shopping for a new pair of oxfords for school. It was a hot summer day and Kristine's feet must have been slightly swollen, though no one thought of this at the time. When the weather cooled off, the shoes turned out to be loose on her feet. Kristine cried that they made her feet look big, and sobbed that she wasn't going to wear them to school. She cried and cried. Dorothy hurried over and took her back to the shoe store. The nervous owner told Kristine walk around in the store wearing the shoes. He carefully examined them, and explained that they had already been worn and he couldn't sell them again, so he couldn't take them back. Kristine had to accept the verdict because Augustina did not have enough money to go out and buy her another pair. And she was with Dorothy, so she couldn't sulk or carry on the way she would have done if she were with her mother. She was stuck with those shoes, and when she wore them to school some of her friends made her feel better when they said her new shoes were really nice. Augustina was relieved.

Kristine would never think of acting sassy when Dorothy was around. She never tried anything with Sig, either, because she knew she didn't stand a chance of getting away with it. But with Augustina, who cared more about her than anybody in the world, she threw her weight around as brashly and thoughtlessly as she pleased. Sometimes when she didn't get her way, she screamed to her mother that she could barely stand her. She acted as though Augustina was not good enough to meet her American know-it-all standards.

Augustina continued to receive both the Kansas City Star and the Kansas City Journal, getting one in the morning and the other in the late afternoon. These newspaper subscriptions were extremely important to her, not only encouraging her to improve her English, but keeping her in touch with current events and the sales in local shops. Newspapers were not thick with all the advertisements that have since made their way into the pages. The paperboy would ride up on his bicycle, roll it up, give it a little twist so it would fold a bit and hold together as he tossed it into the subscriber's front yard.

Augustina watched the newspapers for all the sales in the downtown stores. Often, she was able to buy a dress for Kristine from a sales rack for one dollar. She chose clothes a little too big so Kristine would not grow out of them so fast. Kristine grumbled or howled about this, to no avail. Augustina knew she would not be able to afford to buy new clothes very often, and she was very good at hemming and altering them wherever necessary. She chose pretty pastel cotton dresses or bright prints. Augustina always made sure, though her dresses were few, that they were immaculate when Kristine left the house, and her hair was brushed and shiny.

For herself, Augustina always chose to dress in cheerful colors when she went out, never forgetting the awful dark green dress she had to wear on her last day of school when she was a child.

At home she wore serviceable housedresses in which she could comfortably complete her work.

One day, Kristine brought home a school chum, Edna Tressler. The friend looked around in amazement at the housekeeping room where Kristine and her mother cooked, ate and slept. The whole apartment actually included two other rooms that Augustina had rented out to help pay their way. Edna looked at Kristine in wonder, her mouth agape.

"Why, I thought you were *rich*!" she said, referring to the way she always looked so immaculate and well-dressed. Augustina gave Edna a big smile and her daughter a silent, meaningful glance.

Later when they were alone, Augustina told her daughter, "That shows how important it is to keep your clothes ironed and clean!"

Augustina and Kristine began going to double-feature movies on days other than Sundays - their normal movie day – as movies were becoming more and more popular in America in the thirties and forties. Kristine was always looking to see if her father, Art, was in any of the movies, particularly in costume pictures and mob scenes where so many Extras were used, but she never found him. Every Tuesday, the ushers were dressed in epaulets for Dish Night. Their trip to the movies on Tuesday nights got Augustina and Kristine free dishes, one for each of them. They had to arrive early at the show on these nights to make sure to get good seats, since the free dishes drew a large crowd.

In 1934, when Augustina turned forty-four, she was the mother of a 13 year old daughter and a 25 year old son. She looked ten years younger than she actually was. Her hair was still dark brown and her eyes flashing black. With her party days over, she concentrated purely on making a living for her daughter and herself. In the neighborhoods in which they lived during the heart of the Depression, she never met a man who could offer them anything as stable as she herself could provide.

Sigmond was now a full-fledged printer and working steadily. Dorothy and he brought Augustina and Kristine festively wrapped presents at Christmastime. They knew if they got a present from the Boy or Dorothy, it was of the finest quality because they only bought the best of everything. Augustina, on the other hand, bought just what she could afford, which was very little. She gave Sig and Dorothy little tokens as gifts, or sometimes nothing at all. Even on holidays, the Boy didn't stay long, continuing his habit of sitting on the edge of the chair, ready to leap up and go as soon as the opportunity arose. When the presents were exchanged, he was ready to leave, car keys in one hand, Dorothy's coat in the other, motioning his wife toward the front door.

A few years passed, and it was more important than ever for Kristine to follow what she saw as the American way for teenagers to act, leading to more frequent arguments escalating between her and her mother. Augustina worried when Kristine wouldn't listen to her anymore. Kristine wanted to run away but she had no place to go.

She went to the school counselor and told her that her mother couldn't afford to take care of her anymore and she had to find someplace else to live. The sympathetic woman counselor said she would see what she could do. When she called her into her office a few days later, she said she might be able to get her a job at the Girls' Hotel which was not too far from the high school. She could work as a waitress, serving young women who worked and lived at the hotel, and finish the last term she had of high school. Kristine would get room and board and share the room with another girl and $1.50 per week for streetcar fare and incidentals. Kristine was delighted. Her immense problem was solved. But now she had to go home and face Augustina, knowing it would be an awful situation when her mother found out what she had done.

There was a scene. But the counselor had already talked to Augustina who was very hurt. Augustina ultimately agreed that it might be best for a while, although she could feel her daughter slipping away and did not know if she would ever get her back.

While Kristine was away, Augustina worked long hours in a curtain factory in town, saving a little more money as she only had to shop and cook for one. She was lonely and often sat in her living room in the evening after work, trying to read and write and continue to improve her English, but her spirit was deflated during those days and she often quit only after about fifteen minutes.

When Kristine was ready to graduate from high school, Sig and Dorothy bought her a pink satin graduation dress with a pink net satin trimmed coat to go over it. Augustina was deeply moved and grateful for Sig that her daughter could look so lovely on this special day, since she herself would certainly not have been able to afford a dress anywhere near as nice as this one. Everybody at school loved it, including Kristine.

Augustina, Sigmond and Dorothy came to the graduation in the high school auditorium. With pride, Augustina noticed how Kristine beamed from ear to ear in response to the numerous compliments she received on her dress. Her daughter shone like a gleaming star that entire afternoon, and into the evening. Kristine's friend Edna was sad and heartbroken that she had to wear a crepe print dress with a bertha collar that her widowed mother had bought at the Salvation Army, the best that this family with five children could afford. It was a very pretty dress, but Kristine thought it looked like it might have belonged to an older girl.

Two boys asked Kristine out after the graduation. One, Winifred, was sure she would go with him, but dashing, even surer-of-himself Eugene came along, was introduced to Kristine's trio of relatives, and whisked her away to join a group of young grads in celebration of this momentous time.

The evening ended as Augustina, proud of her daughter, worried that her date might try to get fresh with her.

After high school graduation, the chance of Kristine's getting a job looked pretty dim. Although she made it a point to take typing and shorthand classes in school, following Augustina's incessant prodding, she was a terrible typist and her shorthand, though accurate, was very slow. She was timid on the telephone, as they had never had one at home for very long, if at all. And she never had anything to do with businessmen before, let alone work for them. Worst of all, she was only fifteen years old.

Sig even tried to lend a hand to help his sister find a job. She had taken art classes in school, and Sig admired her sketches of school athletes from newspaper photos. Since Dorothy's brother-in-law was an artist for the Kansas City Star paper, Sig said he would show him her work and maybe help her get a job as an artist with the paper when she graduated! This, however, never materialized.

Mrs. Borchert, the Director at the Girls' Hotel, called her into her office and told Kristine that she had arranged for her to stay at the Girls' Hotel and go to junior college in Kansas City.

"You're a smart girl, and this is a wonderful opportunity for you," she said.

Kristine nodded vaguely, not sure how she would like junior college, but was glad she could stay in school.

But Augustina had other plans. She had been mulling over their future for some time and was anxious to get her daughter back. Her job at the curtain factory had come to an end. She told Kristine she could see no future for them in Kansas City. She had been thinking it over and maybe they ought to go to California.

Kristine was thrilled! All the glamorous movie stars were out there! The weather was sunny all the time, and you could go to the beach and swim in the ocean anytime you wanted to! And her father was an actor, and they would go to Hollywood and see him and her granny! Maybe he would even get her into the movies!

"Do you have their address?" she asked eagerly.

Yes, Augustina had it. At least she had the last letter she had received from Drew, with their return address hand written on the envelope.

"I don't know, that Outfit moves around so much they may not even be there anymore," said Augustina.

"But we can find them, can't we?" asked Kristine anxiously.

As for getting the two of them out to California, she didn't even ask how Augustina planned to do it. She knew her mother, and was certain she would find a way.

Chapter Ten

Augustina did not have the money to get them to California on a train or a bus, but she had seen ads in the Personal column in the Kansas City Star put in by drivers offering rides for passengers in exchange for sharing expenses. She told Kristine her plan was to find somebody to take them by car.

One day when she was scanning the paper, an ad caught her eye that fit her pocketbook to a tee. A couple was offering to take two people to Los Angeles, California for the unbelievable price of twenty dollars for both. This was 1937, and twenty dollars bought a lot of gasoline, costing around 20 cents per gallon.

She went to the drugstore and called the number listed in the ad. It turned out to be a couple named Sybil and Jack, who invited her to come to their apartment and talk it over.

At the apartment house, Augustina hesitated outside for a moment, then rang the bell and stepped inside following Jack's gesture. She looked the couple over suspiciously and decided they might be all right. Then she found out why the price was so low. She and her daughter would have to ride all the way to California in the rumble-seat of a 1931 Ford Model A Roadster.

Fortunately, it was July, and they wouldn't have to worry about freezing back there on the long journey to California. Driving at a speed of 45 to 50 miles per hour, the trip would take approximately four to five days to reach their destination.

Augustina decided they should wear hats to protect their heads from the sun. Something that wouldn't blow off in the wind. They settled on rayon print scarves, tied tightly under their chins.

Augustina took a sweater for each, because it could get chilly if they drove through the mountains or desert at night.

They sure couldn't find a cheaper way to get to California! Augustina said she didn't want to throw away her money on busses and trains because they needed all she had when they got to California. The price, along with the couple, seemed to fit what she was looking for, so Augustina accepted, and went home to get herself and her daughter ready.

When Augustina was in the grocery store buying food to take with them in the car so they would have something to start out with at least, she ran into Harley, the why-don't-you-just man (Why don't you just get a car since you have so many garages?) who used to come to her parties.

Learning that she and daughter were taking off for California with strangers, he was aghast. He warned her that sometimes crooks put ads like that in the paper, then when they get the people's money, they throw them out of the car and leave them in the desert or some other isolated place! "They do it all the time, you know!" he said.

Augustina assured him that these people looked all right, but when she walked away, she began to worry.

She telephoned Sig with the surprising news that she and his fifteen-year-old sister were leaving Kansas City. He couldn't believe it. He hurried over as soon as he got off work, also expressing concern over them taking off with strangers.

"They looked like they're all right!" she told him.

"I don't know about that," said Sig. In addition, he was worried about what awaited them in California. They didn't have any place to go there. He demanded to know if she really thought she was making the right decision!

Augustina said there was nothing to keep her and Kristine in Kansas City. Neither one of them had jobs. Maybe they would have better luck in California.

When Sig learned they were leaving the next day – on Thursday - he was disappointed.

"I can't get off work to see you off, and that worries me," he said. He made Kristine write down the names of the couple they were going with, get the license number of the car, and give him the ad in the paper to which they had responded.

"Just in case I need it!" he said. "I suppose they'll take Route 66 to get to California."

Augustina didn't know. "I guess they know the way or they wouldn't have planned this trip," she said.

"Well, find that out and tell me as soon as you have the answer!" Sig said.

"Will you sleep in the car or stop someplace at night?" Sig asked.

Augustina didn't know that either. "But I don't have much money and I'm sure not going to stay in any hotel!" she said.

"Telephone me so I can write down all these things before you go. I won't see you again before who knows how long! Don't forget to call me soon!" Sig said.

They bid each other awkward goodbyes. They weren't used to hugging or touching very much, but they fumbled around and managed to make a little physical contact. Augustina put on an air of bravado to quiet any fears her children might have about the trip. Although Kristine rebelled against her mother's decisions about her clothes and image at school, she trusted her implicitly in matters like this.

Sig made Kristine swear she would write as soon as they got there.

It was hard to do away with all their possessions except for what they could put in two battered suitcases and a big cardboard box that held all Kristine's toys and prized possessions. Augustina knew they would be lucky if *that* much would even fit into the little Roadster.

Also, there was no way of knowing what lay ahead of them in Los Angeles, or how long it would take to find a place to live, so it might be hard to handle even that small amount of baggage. There were so many unknowns up ahead – at this point she decided she would just have to worry about that when they got there.

Most of her furniture from the House was long gone. She kept certain small items together that she valued, in their own little box that she guarded with her life: Walter's photograph and gold pocket watch, a snapshot of herself with Mother's Day cards her daughter had made for her in school, and the newspaper clipping of Kristine when she was burned at the age of five.

Augustina sold what furniture they had left to a crafty second-hand dealer who tried to give her a pittance for everything she owned. Augustina shouted him down, and he grudgingly handed over a few dollars more. She was angry that she could not make a better deal with him, but there was no more time to haggle with the stubborn s.o.b. or call in another dealer.

At the last minute, Augustina had a screaming confrontation with Kristine, because she wouldn't let her daughter take a second large cardboard box that she had lovingly packed with her most prized possessions: a precious pile of movie star pictures she had cut out of fan magazines and exchanged with her school chum Rose; second-hand magazines she had bought, copies of poems she prized, and her own little stories and poems that her close friends had admired.

Screaming that they wouldn't take up any space, she managed to snatch up the poems and little stories, and the term notebook from her English class filled with her short original writings. If she had realized that Kristine was guarding the special notebook that the teacher had admired so much, she would have definitely wanted her to take it along. But in the heat of the argument, Augustina did not understand this.

Kristine would always remember how pleased her teacher looked on that last day of school when she gave a little speech to the class about one exceptionally fine notebook she had received that year. Recognizing the cover of the notebook lying there on the desk in front of the teacher, Kristine sat in her seat with cheeks flaming. Her teacher handed it back to her saying it was the best notebook she had ever received from a freshman student in all the years she had been teaching.

Kristine rebelliously stuffed her prized possessions into a paper sack. Refusing to put them down, she hugged them to her chest, ready to climb into the rumble seat as soon as the couple arrived. Glaring at her, Augustina attempted to snatch the sack out of her hand and throw it out the window, but did not succeed.

Kristine's eyes were still red from crying as she sulkily waited beside her mother, their baggage at their feet, clenching the paper sack filled with the precious notebook of her poems and treasures. On this sweltering day in July 1937, the perspiring mother and daughter were ready to take off on the long, bumpy journey, with no idea *whatsoever* of what lay ahead.

They carried their head scarves in their hands, for it was too hot to put them on as they stood still waiting for the car to arrive. Once they were well on their trip, the wind would savagely blow their hair into their eyes and face, the midday summer sun would beat directly down upon their heads for a large part of each day, and they understood that was the critical time their head scarves would become the most useful.

The decision had been made so quickly, with their arranged ride ready to leave the very next day, that there was barely time for Kristine to stop by and say a quick tear-filled goodbye to a handful of friends and jot down their addresses.

Sybil and Jack drove up with so much stuff already packed in the car that Augustina feared they wouldn't have enough room for hers and Kristine's minimal load. But with efficient re-arranging and re-packing, they successfully loaded the Roadster.

As Jack was re-packing the car and baggage, Augustina asked if they could make a quick stop at the corner Drug Store to call her son to give him all the details of their trip. Jack nodded in agreement.

Kristine climbed into the rumble seat hugging her treasures, and Augustina settled in beside her with her pots, pans, clothing and personal items, including her pocket book. Sybil asked Augustina to give them their money for the trip.

Augustina hesitated, then took out a handkerchief from her purse and unfolded seven one-dollar bills, handing them to Jack. She announced that she would pay the fare in three installments: seven dollars at the beginning of the trip, seven dollars at the midway point, and six dollars when they arrived at their final destination.

The couple was appalled. "You must pay it *all* before we leave!" protested Jack.

Augustina was adamant. She told them she had heard of cases where they dump you out on the road, once they get your money!

"We won't do that!" yelled Jack.

The irritated couple tried to persuade her to hand over all the money, but Augustina stubbornly held her ground. Not only were they afraid she might never pay the other two-thirds of the fare, now they wondered if she even *had* the rest of the money.

Kristine got red in the face with embarrassment. Oh God(!), the things her mother put her through!

But Jack had a job waiting for him in Los Angeles and if he didn't show up in time, somebody else might get it. They had to leave that morning and had no time to look for another paying passenger. Muttering to each other, the grumpy couple got in the front seat and slammed their doors.

With angry feelings all around, the foursome took off in the little Roadster. A hefty breeze came up and blew Kristine and Augustina's hair wildly about. They tried to tie their scarves around their heads, but had to give up when they almost lost them in the wind. They figured they would have a chance to secure the scarves on their heads at the next stop.

It was private back in the rumble seat, and when the wind was not blowing, they could whisper all they wanted to about the couple in the front seat without their hearing them. But when the wind moaned and howled, they had to shout to hear each other, despite the fact they were sitting hip to hip.

In the daytime when the sun was directly overhead, the rumble seat ride was hot as they imagined hell must be. In the late afternoon and evenings, to protect themselves from the strong, cold wind, Augustina and her daughter huddled together in their sweaters and scarves using their body heat to keep themselves as warm as they could.

At night, they parked by the side of the road, Sybil and Jack unfolded and set up their tent for two, and slept next to the car. Tent-less Augustina and Kristine managed to shift around in the rumble seat enough times to find a somewhat comfortable position, providing them at least a few hours of sleep each night.

They drove through the deserts of New Mexico and Arizona where it was brutally hot. They saw a whole new landscape, with cacti and Yucca and vultures with their long crooked necks cleaning up the carcass of a dead animal baking in the sun. Being so close as they passed this scene was hard to endure, yet curiosity kept their heads turned in that direction until they had long passed the disturbing scene.

When the hot, tired travelers pulled into Albuquerque, New Mexico, Jack turned into a gas station and got out to gas up and give them all a chance to go to the restroom. Sybil got out, trying to smooth the wrinkles out of her dress and smooth down her windblown hair. She followed Jack to the rumble seat where he leaned in, holding out his hand to Augustina.

"We're in Albuquerque - at the halfway point," he told Augustina. "Give me the money."

Augustina fumbled in her handkerchief and handed over seven more single dollar bills.

Sybil grabbed the money out of Jack's hand and put it in her pocket. Under her breath she mumbled a snide remark which neither Augustina nor Kristine could catch, but they were sure it was not "Thank you!"

"She ought to be glad to get it," said Augustina, loud enough for Sybil to hear.

Yet the trip was exciting. They were seeing, smelling, and breathing in new and wonderful terrain, unlike any they had ever seen before. Even though the rumble-seat ride was far from plush, it was worth every hardship, since Augustina believed this was their *only* choice to get to California.

At long last they reached the Golden State, which California came to be called somewhere down the line.

On Route 66 in California, between San Bernardino and Los Angeles, they drove down roads bordered by lush orange groves.

In the late afternoon, the tired foursome rolled into Los Angeles. When they saw the big sign that said LOS ANGELES CITY LIMITS, they perked up and cheered.

Sybil said, "Thank *God*, we made it!"

Everybody in the car was in a good mood now. Their journey was nearly at its end. Augustina had made two payments on the trip, and Jack and Sybil prayed she would make the third one without incident.

Augustina and Kristine had gone through cities and towns they never heard of before; seen flat deserts and tall rugged mountains. In the cramped little rumble seat, they sweated profusely in the midday heat, and when dusk turned to night, shivered in the wind and cold.

In spite of all they had to put up with, they were grateful to the little Roadster for getting them safely to their destination. Jack only had to patch six flat tires during their trip. Miraculously, they had managed to arrive without any major altercations between the couple in the front seat and the twosome in the back!

Augustina and Kristine gawked at the streets lined with picture perfect palm trees. The white one-story buildings and homes in California looked so clean compared to the soot-covered buildings in the Midwestern states where remnants from coal used for heating made their way onto the buildings in thin layers of dark soot.

Now the couple faced the problem of depositing Augustina and her daughter in a temporary room somewhere that Augustina could afford. Kristine was so delighted just to be in famous Los Angeles, that *any* room would have sufficed.

Augustina's heart fluttered with anticipation and fear of the unknown. Everything looked, smelled, and felt so different from Kansas City where she had lived for so many years, and where Kristine had lived her entire life.

They drove up and down the palm tree lined streets, past rows of one-story Spanish-style stucco houses, past business and industrial sections, searching for a sign on a modest house advertising rooms to rent. It was late in the afternoon and all four occupants were anxious for the trip to be over.

In the downtown section of the city, they finally located a house with a 'ROOMS FOR RENT' sign outside. Augustina dragged her weary bones up out of the rumble seat, walked up to the door and rang the bell.

A thin landlady with a coarse voice named Sonya, opened the door and noticed the car parked outside, then turned her attention to Augustina and looked her over. She showed her a room on the second floor with a double bed that Augustina and her daughter could share.

Augustina suspiciously checked out the bedding to make sure it was clean enough to sleep on. She wasn't too happy with what she saw, but she grumbled and took the room for one night. She paid cash, counting out the money in the hall and handing the bills to Sonya, who folded them up and stuffed the money into her brassiere. Sonya handed her the key she had used to unlock the door.

Augustina returned to the car where Sybil, Jack and Kristine waited. She once again took out her handkerchief and carefully unfolded the last six one-dollar bills she owed them, placing them in Sybil's outstretched hand.

Sybil was pleased. She wasn't looking forward to a knock-down, drag-out fight to get that last six dollars. Jack jubilantly extricated their suitcases and boxes from the car and carried them up to the porch, set them down, then went back for the big cardboard box.

Augustina and Kristine started to follow him without saying goodbye to Sybil, but Augustina then changed her mind. After all, the couple did live up to their word and get them to Los Angeles for the price they had agreed upon. She turned to Sybil and bade her a curt goodbye. "And tanks," she added. Embarrassed Kristine nodded and mumbled her own thanks, then hurried after Augustina and Jack toward the porch.

"Where do you want me to put this box?" he asked. "The room is upstairs," said Augustina. "If you could just set it down at the top of the steps."

Jack carried the box upstairs and set it down just inside the door of the room, hurried back down the steps and strode out to the car.

"Say!" Augustina called after him.

He turned with a resigned sigh. "Yes?"

"Tanks," she said. "For all your help."

Caught off guard, he stared at her, then grinned. "Sure," he said, then practically ran out to the car, gunned the motor and sped out of sight with his wife.

The very first night Augustina and her daughter were in L.A., in the early morning hours, they were jarred awake by an earthquake!

Panicked Kristine screamed as the double bed they shared swayed back and forth for a few seconds. The whole thing was over quickly. They held on tightly to the bed, not knowing what would happen next. When the room remained still, they laughed nervously, agreeing this was *some* greeting they got in Los Angeles!

"I hope this doesn't happen all the time!" said Augustina. "I wouldn't want to have to go back to Kansas City in another rumble seat!"

Kristine laughed at the hilarious idea.

They were skittish about lying back down in bed and closing their eyes, but when the room no longer shook for a good ten minutes, they were able to lie back down and get some sleep.

It was cool when they arose in the morning, but it turned out to be hot as the day wore on. There was a hot-plate with one burner in the room, so Augustina was able to make them toast and coffee from the bread and ground coffee she had brought with her. Afterwards, they decided to look up Drew at the last address they had for her from the envelope of the letter she had written a few months before. Kristine couldn't wait to see her Grandma!

On their way to find the landlady to ask for directions to Drew's house, Augustina glanced at a storage shed outdoors with the door ajar, revealing lots of empty space in the clean interior. She made a mental note that this could certainly come in handy with all the belongings she and her daughter had brought with them from Kansas City.

After glancing at the return address on the envelope Augustina handed to Sonya, she told them how to get to Drew's house by streetcar.

As they rode along staring out the window, so happy to be in this famous city, they saw evidence of the Depression in full swing in Los Angeles, just as they had witnessed for so long in Kansas City. People sleeping on the streets, begging for work, asking for money for food. Although this was a distraction to them, they were terribly excited to be in this wondrous city, eager to discover what lay ahead.

Chapter Eleven

In a rundown section of town on the east side of Main Street, they found the address on a two-story stucco building divided into flats each having their own individual addresses.

Augustina knocked on the door matching the numbers they sought. There was no answer. She knocked again. Still no answer. Kristine knocked, and didn't get an answer either. Disappointed, they turned to leave. Just then, an old Ford Touring car drove up the street and stopped in front of the house. A man with tough lined, sun-browned skin got out of the car, a hand-rolled cigarette dangling from one side of his mouth.

Augustina nudged Kristine. "That's Wade!" she said, breaking into a smile.

"My *uncle?*" asked Kristina, amazed. "Yeah!" said Augustina.

Wade sauntered up the walk, looking at them curiously. "You lookin' for somebody?" he asked.

"Yeah," said Augustina, smiling.

Wade came closer. At first, he had no clue as to who they were. Then a look of puzzlement came to his face and squinting his eyes, he took a closer look. His mouth dropped open. "*Augustina?*"

Her smile broadened and he realized this was indeed his ex-sister-in-law. Wade broke into a happy shout, "Augustina!" He ran the rest of the way up the walk and threw his arms around her, giving her a big, long kiss on the cheek. She chuckled with embarrassment.

When he heard that the pretty girl beside her was Kristine all grown up, he was amazed. He embraced her so tightly he squeezed the breath out of her. She gasped for air.

"I can't believe it! I just can't believe it!" he cried. "When did you get out here?"

They told him they just got into town the night before.

"And you found your way here all by yourself!" he said, pleased. They all laughed together, giddy in the moment.

"We knocked on the door but nobody answered," said Augustina.

"Ma's up on Fifth Street," said Wade, "Selling her flowers just like she did in Kansas City! Let's walk up and find her. She's just a block away!"

Kristine perked up expectantly, remembering the Christmas boxes Granny used to send her when she was a little girl. She remembered how some of the cardboard boxes used to arrive torn and crushed, with almost all the Christmas ornaments broken inside. She remembered the "cheap little dresses" Granny sent that were all she could afford. But Granny's heart was overflowing with love for Kristine, even if her son never sent his own daughter a dime. And Augustina had her own thoughts about those packages from California – how she was always disappointed that Art never included a five-dollar bill or anything else to help her support Kristine in their struggle through the Depression.

Up on Fifth Street, evidence of the Depression once again surrounded them. There was a bar with a sign in the window saying 'Cappy's Bar and Grill,' several small stores and shops, and a Midnight Mission where homeless men, wearing shabby suits and felt hats, were fed and sheltered and had to listen to religious sermons. No matter how down and out they were, or how drunk they were, they hung onto their pride, dressing the best they could every time they arrived for their meals. One such man came walking down the street toward them, a little wobbly on his feet, with no acknowledgement whatsoever of their presence, opened the door to the Mission and went inside, confirming the fact he was a regular in that establishment.

Wade spotted his Ma coming toward them from down the block, carrying a basket of artificial flower bouquets she had made in several different colors. In one hand, she carried a small red bouquet. Augustina noticed that her legs were more bowed than the last time she saw her, and her once-brown hair was white now and wind-blown in the breeze that had just come up.

Drew hadn't seen them yet. With twinkling eyes, Wade took Kristine's arm in his, and told Augustina it would be fun to play a little joke on his mother. He asked her to stop a minute and let him and Kristine walk ahead to meet Ma and surprise her.

When Drew caught sight of her son holding the arm of a pretty young girl on the street, she scowled at him. She feared the child was some wayward minor that Wade had just picked up. Jailbait! Wade could get into serious trouble for a stunt like that! Drew knew he liked the girls, but this was going too far!

Wade grinned mischievously, saying to his mother, "I want you to meet a friend of mine."

Drew's lip curled as she gave her son the stink eye, looking the girl up and down disdainfully.

Smiling, Augustina caught up with them and paused beside Wade. With his free hand he reached over and took her by the arm, too, in the same manner he was holding Kristine's.

"Do you know who this is?" he asked his Ma, grinning.

Confused, Drew studied Augustina for several moments before a glimmer of recognition appeared in her widened eyes. "*Augustina*? Is that *you*?" she inquired. They all started laughing.

Tickled, Wade chuckled with delight at his prank, introduced Kristine as her little granddaughter that she hadn't seen in over ten years.

Drew sucked in her breath and examined the pretty young face before her. The scene was overwhelming. She burst into tears and set her basket of flowers down on the sidewalk. Still clutching the red bouquet in her hand, she ran over to Kristine and threw her arms around her.

"You look just like your daddy!" she cried, hugging her as if she would never let her go.

Sobbing, she told them that Art had died just three months earlier. Augustina couldn't believe it. "But he was younger than me!" she said.

Wade nodded solemnly. "He was forty years old. You never know." They all grew somber thinking how sad it was that Art could not have lived for another three months to be there with them that day. Kristine frowned with disappointment. Drew saw her face and squeezed her hand in sympathy. "He always called you his little angel," she said. A sob and a fresh flood of tears flowed from the saddened grandmother.

"What did he die from?" Augustina asked.

"His liver gave out," sobbed Drew. "He had a bad liver."

They fell into another silence. Wade finally broke it with a sigh. "Why don't we all go over to Cappy's and sit down and have a cold beer or a fresh cup of coffee or whatever you want. Treat's on me."

Drew wiped her eyes and picked up her basket of flowers from the sidewalk, following the others inside the bar.

As they distributed themselves around a bare wooden table, Drew took Kristine's hand and pulled her down into the chair next to her. She put her basket of flowers on the floor near her feet and wiped her eyes again, then hugged Kristine some more.

Wade ordered drinks of choice for all. After the mood lightened a little, Wade said, "Augustina, you don't talk nearly as broken as you used to."

"No, you don't," said Drew.

"And you're still just as pretty as you ever were!" said Wade.

Though it was nice to hear their compliments, Augustina thought she would rather have had a few dollars to help support Kristine through all the years Art didn't send a dime.

"I can drive you around this evening if you want to see a little of Los Angeles," said Wade.

"I want to see the beach!" said Kristine.

Wade broke out in a big smile. "All right," he said. "I'll take you and your mother to Redondo Beach."

"You *will*?" asked Kristine, as though he was offering to take them to Mars or some crazy amazing place.

He assured her he would. Augustina wanted to see the beach, too.

Drew wiped her eyes again, then invited Augustina and Kristine to stay with her in her two-room kitchenette apartment until they found a place for themselves. There wasn't much room, but they could squeeze in for as long as they wanted to. Augustina accepted, thinking, "Why not?" She sure had accommodated that whole damn outfit long enough when she had the House back in Kansas City!

She explained that they needed to go back to the room they rented the night before and get their suitcases and a big box.

"How big is it?" asked Drew. When she learned how large it was, she worried she might not have enough room in the small apartment for so much baggage. Wade didn't have too much room either in the small rented house he and his wife Beulah lived in with their seventeen-year-old son, Earl. Wade promised to try and find a spare corner somewhere for her box. Augustina looked at him doubtfully.

Drew went back to work selling her flowers, hoping it would be a good day for her so she could bring home something special for them all for dinner.

Wade drove Augustina and Kristine back to get their belongings. They picked up the suitcases, and placed other odds and ends into the large cardboard box, including Kristine's term notebook and poems and writings, that they knew they would not be needing in the immediate future. Augustina explained to the landlady that there was no room for the large box in the place they would be staying for a week or so, and could the landlady, Sonya, keep the box for them until they found their own place? "We noticed you have a storage shed and thought the box might not be in your way there."

"Sure, leave it here!" she answered in her coarse voice. Grateful Augustina thanked her.

That evening, Wade and his five passengers – Drew, wife Beulah, son Earl, Augustina, Kristine - squeezed into Wade's creaky old Ford, and Wade drove them to Redondo Beach. There were three in the front seat and three in the back. Earl, seated in the back left, looked out the window and didn't say much, feeling awkward about this reunion with his 'relatives' whom he really did not remember. Drew sat between Wade and Augustina in the front seat, with Kristine behind mother and Beulah in the back middle seat. Both Augustina and Kristine stared out the window, mesmerized by the California beauty, whose splendor they could never have imagined.

Her Aunt Beulah tried to get Kristine to bring along a sweater because she said the ocean breeze could really get sharp in the evenings at the beach. But Kristine couldn't believe it would cool off so much after such a hot day. She shook her head. "I won't need it," she told Beulah with confidence.

"You're as stubborn as your mother!" retorted Beulah.

Earl showed a lot of interest in Kristine, peering at her and half-smiling every chance he got. He knew he was adopted and she wasn't his real cousin, so there was no reason he shouldn't stare at her if he wanted to.

Kristine thought he was cute, but she sure didn't come all the way out to California just to date her cousin. She didn't know what to say to him, so she just kept babbling to Wade about how fascinated she was by the beach, the smell of the ocean, and those tall, beautiful palm trees swaying in the wind.

Wade was having the time of his life acting as guide and host to the whole crowd on this exhilarating occasion.

They moved in with Drew for two weeks.

Wade and Beulah lived several blocks away in a small house with two old cars in the side yard, a few blocks from the high school that Earl attended.

In the following week, Augustina found a four-room unfurnished upstairs flat not far from Drew's house. It had a central hallway, so she could rent out two of the rooms. It was a half-block from a business street with a streetcar line, which pleased Augustina, for now they could get around without having to rely on Wade or anyone else to give them a ride.

Her next task was to look for second-hand furniture to furnish the rooms appropriately for sleeping rooms, so she could rent them out and bring in some income for the two of them.

Wade drove Augustina back to get her box from Sonya. The woman said she didn't know how, but the box had disappeared from the storage room. When they protested vehemently that it was impossible, she took the three of them to the storage shed to see for themselves. The shed was empty. Augustina was furious. Kristine was in shock. All her precious stories and poems and mementos were gone!
The woman shrugged and walked back to the house with the three following her in loud protest. The woman reached the house and stepped inside and turned to face them, barring the door with her body so they could not get in.

Calmly she told Augustina, "You got no business having more than you can take care of!" She slammed the door in their faces.

Wade banged on the door, shouting loud enough to be heard a block away, until she opened it again. He demanded to come inside and search her rooms. She said she didn't know what happened to the stuff and shouted for them to get out. She slammed the door again and they heard the key turn in the lock. Wade tried the door and it would not budge. With Augustina shouting angrily, Wade banged on the door until he finally gave up, disgusted.

Livid, Augustina demanded that Wade call the police. Wade explained that he couldn't do that, because he had two or three unpaid traffic tickets, and stirring up the police was the last thing in the world he wanted to do.

"I should have known I couldn't depend on you!" Augustina told him bitterly. She turned around and stormed toward the car with stunned Kristine following.

Feeling part guilt, part shame, that he had disappointed his sister-in-law, Wade hurried to catch up with his family. Augustina said this just proved there are a lot of rotten people in the world! This was just another reason a person had to take care of themselves and *never* trust *anybody else* to look out for them! Now they had to replace all their household items; never mind all the personal belongings that could *never* be replaced despite all the money Augustina could ever imagine having her entire life.

Wade dropped Augustina and the suitcases off at the new apartment, where Drew waited to help get Augustina settled. As Augustina began to unpack what they would need for the next few days, Wade told Kristine he wanted to take her to "get an ice cream soda." Instead, he took her to meet her half-sister whom she had never even heard about! Wade said the girl was three years younger than she was. Puzzled, Kristine couldn't see how that could be.

When the girl's prim-looking mother opened the door and Wade told her who Kristine was, the shocked woman was so furious that smoke nearly shot from her nostrils. How awkward and inappropriate that Wade bring this girl to her front door. Was he *crazy*?

Her curious thirteen-year-old daughter, Marilyn, sidled up behind her mama to see who was at the door. The woman pushed the girl back, then let out a few clipped words to Wade and stood stonily guarding the door so he and Kristine could not make their way into the house. Wade blurted out to Marilyn that Kristine was her half-sister. The bewildered girl stood staring at Kristine, open-mouthed, speechless. Kristine, who barely had her own bearings, thought Marilyn looked pretty stupid with her jaws hanging open like that. The furious mother managed to get control of the door and slam it shut.

Back at Drew's apartment, Kristine told Augustina about Marilyn. Augustina was astounded.

"They sure kept *that* quiet!" she said. Shaking her head, "What an outfit, what an *outfit*!" she said. But she had too many other things to figure out now, and she couldn't let the news of Art and his carryings-on get in the way of sorting out her new life in Los Angeles.

Next day, Wade told Kristine that he went back to Marilyn's house afterwards and her half-sister said of her, "She's *darling*!" Her mother pressed her lips together and managed to get the door closed between them. Upon hearing this, Kristine thought it over and decided that Marilyn was actually a lot smarter than she had appeared at first.

A second-hand store delivered all the used furniture Augustina could afford to the second-story apartment she had rented, and she directed the delivery boy to put the furniture into the house, room by room. Their new apartment had two extra rooms Augustina would rent out to bring in an income. And the best part was the balcony, which brought a smile to her face because she could put out a row of potted plants and have all the beautiful flowers she wanted. Cheerfully, Thursdays would become her watering day. She phoned Sig to assure him they were all right and give him their new address.

It was quite a job to get the rooms in order; swept out and scrubbed, beds made, curtains hung, water pitchers filled on the dressing tables, and all the amenities in place for each room she would rent out. With Kristine's reluctant help, the rooms were finally finished. Augustina put out a sign, 'SLEEPING ROOMS FOR RENT.'

Only a few days went by before a tall, lean, working man with two suitcases came along and rented one room. Augustina cheerfully accepted the cash he paid for the first week's rent. It was a solid start toward paying expenses for herself and Kristine until the girl found a job.

Augustina left the 'FOR RENT' sign out in front, and not a week later, secured a tenant for the other room as well.

Kristine's sixteenth birthday party was held at Granny's house. She was a very young sixteen, hardly grown up enough to go out looking for the office job that Augustina dreamed of her getting.

Drew sent her boyfriend, Conrad, whom everyone called Conny, out to buy a carton of strawberry ice cream and a small white Dolly Madison cake so they could celebrate her birthday. Conny was a tall, lanky man of seventy, with loose false teeth. He blinked a lot, but was a 'good egg,' as Drew would often refer to him.

Drew apologized because she didn't have candles to put on the cake, and Augustina said that didn't matter. Drew said Wade was supposed to come over, but she guessed he couldn't make it, and Kristine was looking so hungry for that cake and ice cream that Drew went ahead and cut the cake and dished it up for the four of them. Nobody objected to the mismatched spoons and dishes they had to use, or the fact that there were no presents. It was Depression time and few people had money to buy gifts. The party guests dug into their sweet treats and relished them, especially the birthday girl.

CHAPTER TWELVE

Kristine looked in the Help Wanted Female columns in the Los Angeles Times newspaper. She had little confidence in her scant office skills, and executive-types such as the people she would be working for were intimidating, as she had never really known anyone, nor spent any time, with people of this caliber. Nevertheless, she landed a job, in fact, she landed several jobs, because she was unable to hold onto one for more than a few days or a week at the most, and Augustina kept insisting that she go out and find another one. The pay was small, but it cheered her mother up and gave her hope for not only her daughter's future, but that of her own.

At this age, Kristine bore a striking resemblance to the actress Judy Garland. Kristine, just one year older than the actress, was beautiful, carried herself with confidence, and always made it a point to look impeccable when she left the house in the morning, a habit she acquired from her mother so many years before in grade school.

The bosses were often paunchy cigar smokers, and the smoke made Kristine give a little cough now and then. One man sat at a desk directly behind her, puffing on his cigar, barking out orders that she nervously tried to follow. When she had to use the restroom, she was afraid to leave her desk, for fear he would fire her if she didn't return quickly enough.

When she answered the telephone, Kristine often got the names of the callers wrong, and was afraid to ask them to repeat their names more than twice. Consequently, she wound up giving incorrect names to her bosses, who frequently blew up and dismissed her as soon as they could find a replacement. It wasn't that she was unqualified for the jobs – on the contrary, she was extremely bright - it was that she did not take a serious interest in working.

Sometimes her bosses would chase her around the desk trying to cop a feel, and this prompted her to quit right on the spot.

Thus, she was often out of work, putting the responsibility back on Augustina to continue supporting the two of them.

After a few months of this, Kristine pleaded with Augustina to let her go to Poly High School where Earl attended, to take an adult course to learn more about office work and maybe in a year when she turned 17, this would help her get a better job. Augustina was not crazy about the idea since she already needed help paying their current bills – without extra tuition costs, but she grudgingly consented. Education had always pulled on her heartstrings, and Augustina realized it would be foolish to pass up this opportunity for her daughter to gain an even greater skill-set and land a higher paying office job. Kristine was ecstatic.

When one student in her class heard the neighborhood she lived in, he made a cutting remark that sensitive Kristine would never forget. He belittled her street, saying that it was on the wrong side of town. Kristine, always making a huge effort to look her best and fit in, never would invite any school friends to her house after that remark. It also reinforced the fact that Kristine always felt everyone else had it better than her. That was certainly not the case, being in the midst of the Depression, where most families, if not all, in her school, were struggling as much as Augustina. However, being the sixteen-year-old that she was, Kristine would not take the chance of being embarrassed about where she lived, so after-school hops and fun with a group of kids always took place elsewhere.

After Kristine finished her courses, Augustina had a falling out with Drew and the family - the last straw - and it was finally clear that she needed to cut that Outfit from her life once and for all.

Augustina was ready to begin her new life in Los Angeles, and definitely did not need that kind of nonsense dragging her down. Reluctantly, she gave up their apartment with the two rentals when she found a smaller one in a different neighborhood that Kristine thought was better. She and Kristine moved away without telling Drew where they went, hoping they would never again run into her ex-in-laws.

They found a modest one-room apartment, once again forced to pare down their belongings in order to fit everything into their tiny living space. But at least they were moving up in the world – looking on the bright side, they were in a better part of town - and Kristine would no longer be so embarrassed to tell anyone who asked where she lived.

It wasn't until Kristine was eighteen that she finally got a real job. Since she wasn't getting anywhere trying to keep a "normal" job, Kristine decided she might as well apply for the kind of job she really wanted - in a movie studio! The mere act of *inquiring* about a job would at least get her inside the studio to fill out an application, and that in itself would be a thrill!

Miracle of miracles, movie-struck Kristine managed to get an interview with the personnel director of Columbia Pictures in the heart of Hollywood. She failed the typing and shorthand tests, but she was so convincing that she would be great at any other office work, that they gave her a chance to work in the file room. Her salary was at the bottom of the studio wage scale, but it was more than she got in her previous little on-again-off-again, chase-me-around-the-desk jobs.

Kristine was glowing when she left the studio after that interview and took the streetcar home. At last she would be close to the glamour she had admired all her life on the screen! Maybe her own *father* had worked at that studio as an actor! Maybe she would meet some of the movie stars whose pictures she used to cut out and save from the magazines!

She sat down and wrote to her friends Edna and Maxine and Mary Catherine back in Kansas City telling them about her great fortune. She knew they would be ooh-ing and ah-ing with envy when they got the news.

But when she actually started working at the "big important studio," she found herself stuck away in a large, bleak room in a dusty gray frame building with other file clerks among many, many filing cabinets. It was far away from the glamour and excitement of the film production going on in other parts of the studio. The lady boss of the file department warned Kristine that she was not to try to get onto any of the movie sets or she would be fired.

Fired! Kristine did not understand!

She learned that, if on her way to or from her dingy work place, she happened to catch a glimpse of one of the celebrities she had expected to be rubbing elbows with daily, she was not to bother them. Bother them? Kristine was crushed. She swallowed hard. Maybe she'd made a mistake taking a job where she would be hidden away in a file room.

But she couldn't quit, or her mother would kill her. Kristine diligently learned to file. She was slower than most of the other girls, since she really didn't take a genuine interest in the work, but she tried her best to be accurate, which some of the faster filers did not bother to do.

There were archives of contracts (the active business files were under lock and key in the Business Department offices,) Story Department files, business documents, accounting ledgers, but what Kristine loved to file most were movie scripts. There were finished scripts and revised scripts, and she was absolutely thrilled to be holding these 'documents of gold' between her fingers!

When she got her first paycheck and they didn't fire her the way they did at all the other jobs, she knew it wasn't a mistake. If she could go to the bank regularly and put money in a savings account, it would be wonderful, and certainly worth it. Kristine had learned from her mother to be careful how she spent her money. She contributed a certain amount from her small salary, which seemed large to her, toward their food and utility bills, and opened a savings account at a bank within walking distance of the studio. She deposited five dollars each week when cashing her paycheck. Augustina's example, coupled with the lesson she learned in elementary school by bringing in her dime each week to put in the bank, taught Kristine a habit she would keep throughout her life. No matter how much or how little she made, the first thing she did when payday came was to put a portion of her check into her savings account.

She had to dress up to look attractive for work so she could keep her job. She bought pretty, inexpensive dresses at the Newberry's Five and Dime that showed off her slim young figure and wore bright red lipstick that Augustina said looked like a smear of blood. But her mother couldn't control her makeup now – after all, she was eighteen! Kristine's golden brown hair shone beautifully each time she left for work, because before bed each evening, she brushed a hundred strokes until it gleamed.

For her own makeup, Augustina was content to simply wear face powder and rouge on her "chicks." She still had her beautiful, smooth complexion, only slightly less rosy than when she first came over from the Old Country.

A young man named Arnold who worked in the studio mailroom began flirting with Kristine when he came in to deliver the mail. He was a sharp-looking 24-year-old who wore a dark blue suit and glasses and acted like he didn't plan to be in the mail room long. A few times he asked Kristine to go out after work for a bite to eat, but she couldn't tell if he was joking around, so she never said yes.

One day when Kristine was talking to two file room coworkers, one of them asked where she lived. When she told them, their eyebrows shot up. The young man shook his head, clucked his tongue, and said, "That's just around the corner from where all the street-walkers hang out.

Kristine's face turned a bright red. "I never saw any street-walkers!" she said sharply. She stomped over to the files and furiously began filing her stack of papers. She was dumbfounded because she thought their new apartment was in a better part of town. She was horrified to think what they would have said if they learned about the neighborhood she used to live in.

Another girl, her best friend in the filing department, told her not to mind that clod. He seemed to know so much about it that he probably hung out there himself! Kristine managed to crack a smile, and choked out a little laugh.

Then Arnold asked Kristine again to have dinner with him, that Friday evening, the next day. She hesitated, then offered to meet him at the restaurant, but he wouldn't go for that.

"I'll pick you up at seven," he said. "Where do you live?" He took out a pen and pad of paper and prepared to write. The two people who had been shocked the other day to learn where Kristine lived, turned around in their chairs, waiting for her answer, watching and listening intensely. Kristine wished she could just sink into the floor or die some other quick way. She couldn't find the words to speak.

"Come on!" said Arnold. "I got to get this mail delivered before I get fired. "Where do you live?"

She hesitated, then taking a chance, reluctantly recited her address, including both the street and apartment number.

"I don't know where that is, but I'll find it," said Arnold as he hurried out.

She was afraid he would, and she looked worried. The two uncouth coworkers were still staring at her. Her best friend came over and comforted her.

On Friday night, Kristine got all prettied up, with her very concerned mother keeping an eagle eye over her as she put on her eye makeup and rounded out her dolling up session with her favorite shade of crimson lipstick. Augustina hoped that her "date" was a nice boy who would treat her daughter with respect. Kristine said, "Oh, Mom, he works at the *studio*. There's nothing to worry about!"

When the knock came at the door, Kristine nervously picked up her small handbag and hurried to answer it. She did not open the door all the way, hoping Arnold would not see too far into their one-room apartment and discover the way she lived. They had no upholstered furniture or pretty drapes, only see-through curtains over the aging green pull-down window blinds.

Augustina knew that Kristine would not invite Arnold in, so she moved toward the door, anxious to get a look at the young man and see if it seemed safe for her daughter to go out with him. As far as she was concerned, Arnold was the enemy from the snooty part of town. When their eyes met, she shot him a suspicious look. Kristine saw him flinch, hastily introduced Augustina as her mother, and rushed him away.

"Whew!" said Arnold, when they stepped out into the street. "Did you see the look she gave me?"

Kristine forced a strangled little laugh. "Oh, don't let that bother you," she said. "She's just like that."

Arnold could not understand how Kristine could live in that location. "I didn't even like coming down here myself!"

Kristine swallowed hard and her face flushed. "We're not planning to live here very long," she lied. As she spoke, she felt the pit of her stomach tighten, for it was terrible to have to make up excuses about where she lived. That whole incident lasting about a minute and a half shattered her expectations of a happy evening with Arnold.

He took her to a modest restaurant where they both had hamburgers. She didn't feel much like talking, so Arnold had to take charge of the conversation. He mentioned a job he was hoping to get as a production assistant and said he had several irons in the fire at other studios. She admitted she wanted to be a writer. He joked that when he was a big producer, she could submit stories to him. Under different circumstances, Kristine would have found that very exciting, but she was sick with worry about what he would tell the people at work. All she could think of now was ending the evening as soon as possible.

Arnold turned out to be a nicer guy than she had given him credit for. He knew she did not live there by choice and she was nice girl, really. Answering questions from people at work about their date and any subsequent relationship, he said, "She's a nice girl, but we don't have much in common."

"You mean too nice," asked the guy in the file room, suggestively.

"I didn't say that," snapped Arnold, and he walked away without ever bringing up mention about where she lived. He liked Kristine and he thought she was pretty, but he had high expectations about his career and didn't think she would add much to his plans.

From then on when Arnold delivered mail to the file room, Kristine made it a point to be absorbed in her work. Or she would leave the room if possible. Once when he tried to talk to her, he got the "cold shoulder." He didn't bother her anymore and never asked her out again.

A few months later, he left the mailroom for a job as a production assistant trainee at another studio. Kristine bumped into him in the hall and congratulated him with mixed emotions. "Well," she said, "Your dreams are coming true even if mine aren't." But at least she didn't have to worry about being so uncomfortable around Arnold anymore. He impulsively gave her a quick kiss on the lips. She never saw him again, but she saw his picture in the paper once at a film preview after he got married.

Kristine begged her mother many times to move. She called it a miserable neighborhood. She was ashamed to bring anybody home!

Augustina said her friends were no good if they didn't like where she lived. "Is that why that guy didn't come back?" she asked. Kristine sunk her head low, looking at her shoes, and reminded herself how grateful she was that "that guy" had not spread her address around the office, exposing her questionable neighborhood to the entire work crowd. She didn't answer her mother, but Augustina knew how her daughter felt about their living situation.

Augustina got very angry at her lack of understanding. With Kristine's record of quitting jobs, Augustina was afraid to give up the security of living in an affordable neighborhood until she knew for sure that Kristine would remain employed long enough to contribute her share to their monthly expenses. Kristine had quit so many jobs, and who knew how long she would hold onto the job in the file room? After Augustina bought the furniture she needed when she came to California, in addition to replacing all the household items that were in the box that Sonya stole when they first arrived, she had little savings left. The apartment that Kristine was so ashamed of, was a place where Augustina could pay their rent and take care of them until Kristine could make more money. She rightfully felt her daughter should consider herself lucky that her mother had always managed to support them both without having to ask anybody else for help.

Oh, how Kristine was waiting for the day she could convince Augustina to move to a nicer apartment where she wouldn't be ashamed to bring her friends. Otherwise, she might have to move out on her own, if that was the only way she could live in a better part of town, but that would take a lot more money than she had right now.

After another big argument with Augustina about where they lived, a new girl named Lynn came to work in the file room. Lynn lived with her parents in Santa Monica, and had a long commute to Hollywood on the bus each way. Kristine listened with interest as Lynn told another girl that she was looking for a roommate so she could move closer to the studio.

On their lunch break, Kristine approached Lynn and said she, too, was thinking of moving out on her own. "I'm living with my mother now, and our apartment is too small for both of us."

Lynn was delighted. She asked Kristine how her mother felt about her moving out. Kristine managed to stammer that they hadn't discussed it yet. She didn't want to lie to Lynn the way she had lied to Arnold when she told him they would be moving from that place soon, and she *was* going to talk to her mother just as soon as she and Lynn found an apartment.

They chatted easily and enthusiastically, and it looked as though they would get along fine. Kristine learned that Lynn's ambition was to own her own bakery, that she didn't have a steady boyfriend at the time and neither did Kristine. Lynn suggested they try to find a reasonably priced apartment within walking distance of the studio.

Kristine laughed. "That sounds a lot like what my mother would say. She'll like you."

But Kristine felt as though she was doing something wicked by going behind Augustina's back in planning to move out. She decided not to say anything yet to Augustina. She would wait and see if indeed they *could* find a place she and Lynn could afford before she broke the news to her mother.

The two girls began scouring the area for apartments on their lunch hour. They could hardly believe their luck when they stumbled upon an attractive single furnished apartment in a two-story apartment building, with a pull-down Murphy bed that they could roll into a giant closet every morning. The closet also had a dresser and several clothes racks – perfect for two girls! – and, there was a fold-out couch in the living room. They loved it! By splitting the rent and food money, it would be affordable for them both. Kristine sat down on the couch and bounced up and down on it a few times. "This is really comfortable!" she said. She volunteered to be the one to sleep on it.

The woman manager, Mrs. Whitman, said she had a daughter living with her who was a few years older than Kristine and Lynn. After they told her they wanted to rent the apartment, she talked to them for a half-hour or so, casually sizing them up without their realizing it. She asked them where they were from, where their folks lived, etc. She emphasized that all her tenants either worked or went to school, and they had to be quiet after 10 p.m.

"You girls are very young," she said, and they worried that she thought they were too young. But she smiled and said she had a good feeling about them and decided to take a chance, because they worked at the studio only three blocks away. Although Mrs. Whitman knew that some of the studio people were on the wild side, these two young ladies seemed like nice girls themselves.

They were happy and thanked her. There were smiles all around. They gave her a deposit and she gave them a receipt. From then on, Mrs. Whitman called them "My_Girls."

After Kristine and Lynn said goodbye and went their separate ways, Kristine made a trip to the W.T. Grant Variety Store and bought a large inexpensive suitcase. She didn't want to move into the new apartment with the old beat-up one she had to put her clothes in when they moved out from Kansas City, travelling in the rumble seat of that Ford Roadster.

When she arrived home lugging the big suitcase, her heart was thumping. Now she *had* to tell her mother.

Augustina was stirring a thick homemade soup with meat, potatoes, carrots, and celery in a steaming pot on the stove. It would be their supper. The enticing aroma reached Kristine's nose, making her feel guiltier than ever.

Her mother turned, stunned to see Kristine set the big suitcase down on the floor. "What's that?" she demanded, afraid to hear the answer.

"We found an apartment today," said Kristine simply.

Augustina became fiery angry. "Who's *we?*"

With resentment, she exclaimed now that Kristine finally had a steady job, instead of helping her out, she wanted to move in with *another* thoughtless girl who had also left home!

Kristine shot back, "It's a friend from work, Lynn, and she's not thoughtless. In fact, she is extremely reasonable and responsible. I told you over and over I want to get away from this part of town and you won't go!"

Augustina angrily turned off the fire under the soup pot. Breathing heavily, she went to the table and sat down on a chair. Kristine picked up the suitcase and carried it to her side of the double bed and set it down, staring defiantly at her mother. Augustina stared silently at the tabletop. They said nothing to each other for a while, then Augustina stood up. "We better eat while it's hot," she said quietly.

Kristine looked over at her with great compassion as tears filled her eyes.

Augustina knew that Kristine was having a good time sharing the apartment with "that girl," Lynn, and going out with boys. Her daughter could have all the company she wanted now, and not be ashamed to bring them to her snooty apartment. Augustina worried about her constantly.

When Kristine learned that Lynn was going to visit her folks in Santa Monica the following Saturday morning, she telephoned Augustina and invited her mother to come over and see where she lived. Augustina was anxious to see the place but upset that Kristine had taken so long to invite her.

Augustina put her hair up in curlers the night before, the way she always did when she was going someplace special, and wore a white rayon blouse, carefully ironed, and a new print skirt she had recently made, gathered at the waist, taking extra care to make sure her slip didn't show past the bottom of her skirt. Picking up her pocketbook, she left, turning the key in the Yale lock on her apartment door she had installed when she moved in. She crowded into the streetcar with standing room only, then transferred twice and arrived on Kristine's front porch right at 10:00 a.m., the agreed upon time.

She knocked on the door and Kristine, wearing shorts and a wide-necked peasant blouse, smiled as she let her in. Kristine looked flushed and happy.

"Come in, Mom!" she said cheerfully.

Two tennis rackets stood against the wall. Augustina realized with a pang that Kristine was having a lot of fun now that she was away from her. She stepped inside and looked the apartment over with a critical eye and bluntly told her daughter that she didn't think it was so hot. Kristine rolled her eyes. Her mother said exactly what she expected her to say, and there was no point in arguing about it. Kristine knew she could never win anyway.

Augustina was uneasy at first, being out of her comfort zone, then agreed to sit down just for a little while. She asked where her roommate was, and Kristine explained she was in Santa Monica visiting her parents.

She was pleasantly surprised when Kristine asked her to stay for lunch. Kristine took out some bread and cheese and lunchmeat from a small apartment refrigerator that required manual defrosting every week. Then she produced a small jar of Miracle Whip, Augustina's favorite sandwich spread, and held it up for her to see. Augustina was pleased. Smiling, Kristine produced mayonnaise she would put on her own sandwich, and they sat down.

Together they made sandwiches and had lunch. They ate heartily, argued a little bit afterward, then said their goodbyes including Kristine's promise to stop by and see her soon. After Kristine was sure her mother knew her way back home, Augustina left.

Kristine came to visit her mother once a week, usually on Saturday morning. She brought her mother pastries from her favorite family owned bakery, and percolated a fresh pot of coffee. They sat and ate together at the small round table in the kitchen near a window looking out onto the passers-by on the sidewalk. Most of the people they saw were dressed in casual Saturday clothing and walking leisurely, enjoying the flowers in bloom and the beautiful weather, grateful to have the day off from their arduous work week. They would often see an elderly couple slowly stroll by, to whom they would eventually wave and say a friendly "Good Morning."

The year was 1945, and Kristine was 24 years old. Since renting her apartment with Lynn, they had moved a couple of times, getting a larger place and bringing in different roommates, both still working at the studio.

Suddenly there was a massive studio strike with angry, shouting meetings, threats being made, picketing, fights on the sidewalk that escalated to violence, and picketers thrown in jail. Frightened Kristine heard that The Mob controlled IATSE Local 728 and the CSU (Confederation of Studio Unions) among other unions, who called the strike that stopped all film production across Hollywood.

She did not dare go to work and try to cross the picket lines, but she didn't know how she would get by without a paycheck. She didn't have to worry long because with all film-making coming to a sudden halt, she was abruptly laid off along with thousands of studio employees throughout the industry.

A family crisis came up and Lynn moved back to Santa Monica to be with her folks. She promised to contribute her share of the rent to Kristine and the girls one more month but could not promise anything beyond that.

Kristine began to visit her mother more frequently now that she had time on her hands. Augustina still had not made up with Drew and her Outfit, and they no longer visited each other. This meant Augustina virtually had no family around her. Since she did not make friends easily, Kristine's visits became the highlights of her life.

The studio strike threatened to drag on for a long period, and no one could predict when it would come to an end. Kristine was growing ever more restless. She learned that when workers were hired back to the studios, they were called back by seniority. Kristine had little seniority. They wanted her to picket and she was fearful of the violence she had seen. She began working on a plan to determine what she should do with her life in the meantime.

Augustina continued working at a job she found in a curtain factory downtown, scrimping and saving and living very frugally, really the only way she knew how.

Augustina greeted her daughter one day with a letter in her hand, a letter from Sig, whom she still fondly called the Boy.

Sig was now in his thirties and still living in Kansas City. World War II was raging. Sig had not been drafted because of the back injury he had sustained a few years earlier. Augustina remembered receiving a letter a few years ago that mentioned Sig had hurt his back, but she did not realize the seriousness of this injury, and she did not really know all the details of how it happened.

Whenever Sig wrote to Augustina, it took her some time to "make the words out." She called on her daughter to come over and help her answer the letters. She told Kristine what she wanted to say, then copied what Kristine wrote, and "scratched a few words" herself at the end. Sometimes, with Kristine's encouragement, she laboriously wrote a brief note by herself with her often impatient daughter standing by to correct the spelling.

"You ought to go to night school!" Kristine scolded her.

Augustina reminded her that she had tried to do that in the past, but it never worked out.

"Oh, that was a long time ago!" scoffed Kristine. "Before I was born! You shouldn't give up. Not ever!" She announced that she herself was going to go to college one of these days. Augustina stared at her. She didn't think college was necessary, but she stopped herself from discouraging her daughter, the way she herself had always been so many times.

They learned through a letter that Sig and the beautiful Dorothy had married in a quiet ceremony, with only one special couple in attendance, the Hooks, who stood up as their witnesses. Augustina and Kristine had never met the Hooks.

It was a bombshell blow to Augustina. In her eyes, her importance to the Boy had now diminished. But Kristine was delighted to hear the news because she admired Dorothy so much. Finally, Augustina grudgingly admitted that if he *had* to get married, Dorothy was a good choice. And Sig told them that the Hooks' had practically adopted him after Augustina and Kristine ran off to California.

Another letter brought news that Sig had given up the printing trade and become a jeweler. He now owned his own jewelry shop "Out South," as Augustina put it, meaning in the snooty part of town. He enclosed a snapshot of himself and his lovely wife standing proudly outside his store. Dorothy's meticulous dress, impeccable posture, and kind smile complemented her handsome, tall, lean husband.

Seeing her older brother successfully move on in life increased Kristine's restlessness to get something going herself. Since she had no special boyfriend and no prospect of one in the near future, she decided to follow in her mother's footsteps and take off on an adventure of her own. Augustina had started out when she was 18 years old, crossing the European continent, then the

Atlantic Ocean, then finding a husband in New York City and travelling to a new home in St. Joseph, Missouri. Everybody her mother knew told her she was crazy to start out alone like this, but she did anyway.

Now Kristine wanted to try her own luck! She was suddenly bursting with excitement. She would go on an adventurous journey to New York City! Augustina was horrified to hear it.

As Kristine travelled across the county to New York, back in Los Angeles, Augustina worried about her every mile of the way. She was happy when her daughter's fortunes were good, and suffered with her when they were not. With Sig and Dorothy happily married, successful, and living the good life back in Missouri, and no other family besides Kristine, each day became obsessed with Kristine's absence. Basically, Augustina's whole life at this point revolved around the concerns and worries of her daughter's precarious journey.

Augustina had gone out to pick up some groceries for dinner just as it was turning dusk. A burglar, watching her leave, entered her apartment by forcing open the first floor side window. He rummaged around the apartment as night began to fall, not wanting to turn on the lights. Finding a box full of drapery remnants that Augustina had brought home from work, he emptied the contents all over the apartment floor searching for valuables hidden beneath. Realizing there was nothing of value, he became angered and caused more destruction to her home.

When he came across a locked suitcase, certain there were valuables inside, he became frustrated at not being able to break open the lock. He pounded on it, kicked the lock, and swore in a loud whisper. When he heard voices of tenants in the hall, he fled back out the window with the suitcase, leaving the mess of drapery remnants and the rest of the disarray he caused, discarded all over her apartment floor.

Upon his exiting the window, a concerned neighbor immediately sized up the situation, and ran to apprehend the burglar. A fight erupted in the street between the two men resulting in bloodshed, but the burglar got away with the suitcase. Her neighbor was found unconscious when the police arrived along with an emergency ambulance. As Augustina walked up her street carrying a sack of dinner potatoes, carrots, onions, and stew meat, she came upon the scene, directly in front of her house.

To compound the hardship, through the confusion and Augustina's lack of command of the English language, the suitcase was never recovered. Augustina had always kept it locked because it contained her only prized possessions: Walter's gold pocket watch; her onyx earrings and good pearls that Sig had given her over the years; a few trinkets she had collected in her travels such as a snow globe given to her by Jan in Antwerp and a miniature version of the Empire State Building; the portrait of Walter standing solemnly in front of his shoe repair shop in St. Joseph with the intense expression in his eyes; and various snapshots from the time she met Walter on through Kristine's childhood. Also in the suitcase were Christmas and Mother's Day cards that Kristine and Sig had made in school which Augustina highly treasured. Not only the adorable pictures her children had drawn on these precious cards, but the touching sentiments such as, "You are the best mother ever," truly touched Augustina's heart, since all her life she spent striving to be 'the best mother ever' for her beloved children. And the newspaper picture of Kristine at age five with her face and head bandaged from when she bumped the pot on the stove and the boiling water tipped on her head and severely burned her. Augustina felt that the whole world of her past had been stolen away. She never in her entire life felt more alone and frightened.

The theft of this suitcase signified another part of her life had been stripped away, with no possibility of ever gaining it back. The losses over her life, up until her current age of 56, were substantially more than most experience over an entire lifetime. First her mother died when she was 7, then she learned of her little sister Maria's death shortly after Augustina came to America, then her husband Walter's shocking accident, then her friend Charlie's death, next her ex-husband and Kristine's father's death, and now any precious memories of them all gone, gone, gone forever. Little by little Augustina's past was being taken from her, and her unknown future provided no comfort. This left her feeling extremely lonely, frightened, and sick with worry over what misfortune might happen next.

A very distraught Augustina wrote a letter to her daughter expressing downright fear, which was most unusual for Augustina. From across the United States, Kristine was shocked and saddened to hear the news, and felt completely helpless and filled with guilt for leaving her mother alone in Los Angeles.

Though she had procured a job as the assistant editor at Vogue Magazine in Manhattan, this alarming incident brought Kristine back to L.A. Not only because of the concern for her mother's safety, but in addition she had read on the front pages of the New York newspapers that the studio strike had been settled in Hollywood. As much as she loved her job and the big city life, her NY salary was too small to afford her the kind of life she would have loved to live in New York City.

So Kristine returned to Los Angeles, and lived with Augustina for a short time. Now that she was back in town, and Augustina had had time to reflect on her living situation, she announced crisply one evening over dinner that she thought they should move. Kristine could help her settle into her new place, then Kristine could start looking for a place of her own. Kristine was delighted! She was eager to help her mother find a place in a better area, and eagerly promised to help. Augustina said Kristine could help with moving the furniture and packing her belongings, but she wanted to *find* the place on her *own*. Through Kristine's persistence, she accompanied her mother anyway. She wound up talking her into renting an apartment more expensive than she could afford which was totally against Augustina's better judgment. Kristine's reasoning was that she would be safer and better off here, and there would be peace of mind for the both of them. Kristine paid to have telephone service installed for her mother, and told her mother she would pay the bill each month.

Kristine was able to find a reasonable studio apartment for herself, since she landed a secretarial job at another studio.

The new neighborhood was an old one, but Kristine thought it was more "respectable." Augustina was unsuccessful in trying to sublet a couple of rooms, so found it difficult to meet her rent. She blamed the fiasco on her daughter, saying she knew this decision was not sensible to begin with, and only moved here after the constant nagging from her daughter. This lead to a shouting match over the telephone.

She tried to console her mother whose next month's rent was due in a few days. She gave her half of it, which was all the money she had to spare at the time.

Augustina knew she had to find another way to earn her living. Renting rooms had worked well back in Kansas City for a while, and even when she had first moved to California, but times were changing, and she couldn't count on a steady income from that anymore.

She looked in the newspaper and saw an advertisement put in by a school for power machine operators. The ad said that with World War II in full swing, factories were crying for power machine operators to make military uniforms and other army and navy equipment.

Augustina dug into her small bank account and came up with enough money to enroll in the two-week course.

At the end of the course, Augustina was far from being an expert power machine operator, and she was on her own to try and find a job. Due to her continuing lack of fluency in the English language, in particular around specific terminology of cutting and sewing uniforms, she conceded it would be very challenging to get hired. But Augustina knew she had to do something to earn money, so again, she turned to the newspaper, looking in the Help Wanted Female ads.

Augustina applied for a job making Army pants. She was one of three women hired on a Monday, but was too flustered and unskilled to be kept on for longer than Wednesday of that week.

It took a lot of courage for her to wake up the next morning, get washed up and dressed, and get out there to apply for another job. But somehow, she dug deep inside to that eternal strength and never-ending persistence; that will to keep going no matter what, that she had turned to so many times before, and was hired that same day to sew Navy uniforms. Her second job lasted three days. Knowing she absolutely had to bring home an income, she persevered, returning again to the want ads, searching, calling, interviewing until she was hired a third time. This job lasted a week and a half before she was dismissed.

But there were lots more ads in the paper. Power machine operators were so desperately needed at that time that she knew there had to be some job she was good at and could steadily hang on to. Augustina kept her chin up and looked on the bright side. She took short daily walks, admiring the blue California skies with their white puffy clouds and the beautiful orange, yellow and pink flowers planted in her neighbors' gardens. She came to realize that with the experience she got with each job, though short-lived, she was getting better and better. With each new job she landed, she stayed longer than the one before. This gave her hope to keep on trying.

One day she applied at a women's sportswear factory, necessitating the confrontation of yet another interviewer. He was a middle-aged man in shirtsleeves, wearing black-rimmed glasses that although appeared too big for his face, gave him the appearance of being quite an efficient man. As she sat anxiously before him, he said,

"So you're from Kansas City. Ever been around 13th and Troost?"

Surprised, she told him she sure was. She owned a house on Tracy, off of 13th Street.

The man recalled an explosion twenty years before when a house blew up because of a leaky gas main. He was a boy working at the grocery store on the corner at the time.

"I remember!" said Augustina. "Two women were killed."

"No," he told her. "They were hit by flying wood from the house and had to be taken to the hospital, but they weren't killed." He liked her, and Augustina felt that this time, she had a friend on her side.

She was hired, and her new boss did not push her too hard until she had enough experience to produce satisfactory work. She took the streetcar to work until she was confident that they would keep her, then moved to modest quarters nearby so she could walk to work. That job lasted for years. Kristine continued to pay her mother's telephone bill, assuring they could always be in touch.

One day when Kristine came over to see her, Augustina gave her a present of a pretty cotton print sports outfit that the women's sportswear factory was making at the time - a blouse with a shirt-maker collar and matching shorts. She insisted Kristine her try it on and was pleased that she had picked the right size and that it looked so pretty on her daughter.

But Kristine grumbled that she didn't like the collar, so she didn't wear the outfit much. Augustina was hurt. Kristine made it clear that she preferred the wide-necked peasant blouses that were so popular at the time.

With the help of Augustina's mentoring, and the tricks and skills she had learned from her machining jobs, she taught Kristine to be an excellent seamstress. Her attention to detail, pressing them flat after sewing each seam, trimming and clipping the rounded sleeve seams, the meticulous way she hand-sewed the hems and tacked the facing to the darts and sides, resulted in a beautiful and unique wardrobe for Kristine.

Her first sewing project lead Kristine to the F.W Woolworth company to buy a pattern and cotton fabric in three different colors, so she could make herself three beautiful peasant blouses. Her friend had given her a sewing machine when she had moved away, and Kristine treasured it, knowing it would allow her to make more beautiful clothes than she could buy. The peasant blouses' successful outcome was largely due to her mother's mini sewing lessons and detailed instructions as Kristine pinned, cut out, and sewed seams, armholes, and hems, then inserted the elastic around the neckline. Kristine basked in the compliments she got from her friends, but only as an afterthought did she mention that Augustina helped her develop and perfect her sewing skills which enabled her to make such lovely clothes.

It was a touching scene – Augustina now the teacher and Kristine the sewing student – a far cry from years past where Kristine was the English teacher to her pupil Augustina. This was the turning point in years of a challenging relationship between mother and daughter, that is to say, although Kristine knew her mother would always provide for her in the most basic sense, this was the first time she saw her mother as a leader, a mentor, a guide, who knew a great deal more than herself about sewing, and for that matter, a great deal more about life, as well.

CHAPTER THIRTEEN

After that, Kristine began to visit her mother every Sunday. She started mentioning somebody named Bill, a young free-lance actor she met at the studio when he got "a big part" in a low-budget action movie.

Augustina asked blunt questions, like "Free-lance? What's that?" Kristine told her that a free-lance actor was called to fill the role when producers were looking for a specific part.

"What does he do the rest of the time?" asked Augustina.

"Why, he waits for his agent to get him another part!"

"You mean he hasn't got a steady job?" asked Augustina.

Kristine got irritated because Bill was a good actor and it wasn't his fault that he didn't work all the time!

"You mean he doesn't work very much?" asked Augustina. She got uncomfortable when her mother alluded to the fact that Bill didn't work a lot, because it sounded too much like Kristine's father, Art - charming, persuasive, lazy.

Kristine kept insisting that he was an excellent actor and when he got to be a little better known she was sure he would work all the time. "Everybody says so!" she declared.

"A lot of guys who don't work much brag about what they're *going* to do," said Augustina. "I've already met a bunch of those."

That touched off another argument. Kristine said Bill's agent was always out looking for acting jobs for him. She defended her right to decide who she wanted to go out with.

"I don't think you're using your sense," said Augustina.

Kristine declared her mother didn't understand the movie business! There were lots of actors who didn't work all the time, but when they did get parts they made good money. Bill did a lot of plays at the Little Theatre and Pasadena Playhouse plays and he got good reviews for his work! He had shown her some clippings from the newspaper and the reviews all said he was very good! He even got a personal compliment from Gregory Peck who told him he was a great and talented actor after a play they did together at the Pasadena Playhouse!

Augustina was skeptical. "If he's so good, why isn't he working now?" she asked.

"Because the play closed!" said Kristine. "Oh, I'm going home! I have a date with Bill and I have to get dressed!"

What Kristine did not mention to her mother which was also a contributing factor to her attraction to Bill was the fact that he took so much care in keeping himself fit and handsome. Part of his fitness routine included going to Muscle Beach in Venice a couple of times a week to work out with the bodybuilders there, and swimming in the Pacific Ocean, just outside the breakers where he and his buddies could get in a good 30 minute freestyle workout.

"Well, what are you hiding him for?" asked Augustina. "Bring him around so I can get a look at him!"

Kristine frowned. "Okay, I will. 'Bye."

A disappointed Augustina said goodbye to her at the door and closed it carefully. She had a worried look on her face.

"I want to get a car!" Kristine announced to her mother one day. She had almost saved up enough money for a down-payment as well as the insurance she would have to buy, but she didn't know how to drive yet.

"Why do you have to spend all that money on a car?" asked Augustina. "Why can't that bozo you spend so much time with drive you around?"

"I want my own car to drive to work and use anytime I need it. I'll take you for drives, too, Mom. We can drive down to the beach, or go anyplace we want to, as soon as I'm good enough to get a license." Augustina realized that she was actually tickled to hear it.

As soon as Kristine saved up enough money, she signed up for driving lessons from an energetic gray-haired man with a heavy Jewish accent who put an ad in the classified section of the newspaper under 'Learn to Drive.'

Augustina asked why she did that. Couldn't that bozo she was spending so much time with teach her?

"Stop calling him a bozo!" demanded Kristine. "He offered to teach me, but I'd already signed up for lessons and couldn't get my money back."

"Aw, go on," said Augustina with a wave of the hand.

"It's true!" said Kristine. She added guiltily, "Besides, his car isn't running very well right now." She admitted that his Studebaker had broken down in the middle of Doheny Drive the week before, when they were out on a date, and they had to wait until somebody stopped and gave them a push. It happened one more time since then, but that time she wasn't with him.

"It's a good thing," said Augustina. A worried look crossed her face. It reminded her too much of Art and his old cars, and she didn't want Kristine to get involved with anybody that undependable.

"Don't get mad because he's in between jobs, and has to wait until he gets his next check," said Kristine.

"Why can't he just take it out of the bank? He's got a savings account, doesn't he?"

Kristine reluctantly admitted that Bill didn't have a savings account right now.

Augustina was horrified. Art all over again!

Kristine hotly defended Bill, saying he just changed agents and this new one was very good.

When the driving course was finished, Kristine did not pass her driving test.

Augustina was bewildered. "What happened?" she asked.

Dejected Kristine explained there was a left-hand turn she couldn't make. The traffic scared her too much. She was sitting out in the intersection on Santa Monica Blvd. with her left turn signal blinking ready to make a left-hand turn when suddenly she panicked at the sight of cars moving all around her – going past her and coming toward her. Her agitated instructor yelled at her and grabbed the wheel telling her to put her foot on the gas pedal and guided them safely across the street into the right lane. When it was safe to do so, he pulled over to the curb and threw up his hands and yelled at her some more.

"You could have killed us both!" he told her. Since she had paid him in advance, he wasn't concerned about how he spoke to her or what he said. "The lesson is over, and you did *not* pass!"

The next day, a frustrated Kristine let Bill give her a few more lessons and she passed her driving test after a couple of weeks on her second try.

The next step was to get a car. Bill wanted to help her find one, but – oh happy day! – his agent came up with an acting job for him, and he couldn't help her for two weeks. Kristine and her mother went around to dealers' lots and looked at a hundred cars. They agreed that a shiny blue 3-year-old Studebaker coupe that looked brand new was the best one of the bunch. They decided it was smart for Kristine to save the money she had put aside for the car so she would still have money in the bank for unexpected expenses. When Security First National Bank agreed to give Kristine the loan she needed to finance the car and pay for the insurance, they were both thrilled. Her first driving chore was to very carefully drop her mother off at her apartment, then cautiously drive herself home.

Augustina, who never drove a car herself, trusted Kristine behind the wheel implicitly. She was ready in a flash anytime Kristine called her to say she was coming to pick her up, so they could go for a drive.

Their first big trip was driving to Redondo Beach, where Wade had taken them the day after they arrived in Los Angeles. In the daytime they got a much better view of the oil rigs they had seen before when it was dark. It was a happy trip, and Augustina never doubted her daughter's driving skill for one minute. She gazed in wonderment out the open passenger's window at the vastness in the idyllic blue sky and perfectly aligned palm trees along the Coast Highway. She looked beyond the horizon, past the deep blue water and whitecaps swishing playfully around the ocean's surface. She listened to the seagulls and watched them fly in formation many feet above their car, so happily and carefree on their way to somewhere or nowhere. Bill was barely mentioned, but Kristine admitted she was still going out with him. She glanced at Augustina ruefully when she said it. Augustina saw the look and warned her to be careful. Kristine changed the subject and drew in a deep breath of the fresh ocean air, exclaiming how wonderful it was. Augustina agreed, but she shot Kristine an uneasy glance, wondering what was really going on between her gullible daughter and "that bozo."

After Bill's acting job was finished and he got his check, he paid all his bills, mostly for rent and utilities and a cleaning bill. He then took Kristine to a discount department store on La Cienega that catered only to union people who worked in the entertainment industry. It was a furtive trip that they felt both excited and guilty about. Especially Kristine.

They picked out a pretty, modestly priced wedding ring for Kristine, a gold band with a little curlicue scroll design.

Kristine loved how it looked when it was fitted on her slender finger. With a huge smile across his face, holding his broad shoulders tall, Bill agreed. Though Bill was not a tall man – maybe 5'5" – his proud stature and muscular frame always gave the appearance of importance and confidence, making his handsomeness that much more attractive. The jeweler could not help noticing the pride Bill displayed, standing beside the counter with his beautiful bride-to-be, as he counted out and paid in cash for the ring.

The next step was getting the marriage license and waiting the required three days before legally using it. They nervously filled out their papers and got more excited than ever.

Most people in the early 1950's did not have the means to pay for a big wedding without going into debt, and credit cards were unheard of. Simple weddings before a minister or Justice of the Peace were often the norm.

So they arrived at Los Angeles City Hall at 11:00 a.m. on that particular Friday morning in March, dressed up in their finest. Bill wore his most handsome grey suit and a deep blue and grey Art print tie that he often wore on auditions for his acting jobs. Kristine wore a new street-length soft blue crepe dress that she had bought the week before and that she could wear for dressy occasions in the future.

A court employee stood up as their witness as they were married by one of the judges who seemed pressed to get on to the next couple. He was not too much in a hurry, however, to accept the tip that Bill held out to him before he rushed out of their lives forever. By the time the happy, dazed couple stepped outside the courthouse into the bright sunlight, they barely remembered what he looked like.

Kristine's heart beat triple time as she pictured her mother's face when she found out about this. One thing she was sure of: Colorful expletives would rip the air! Words, she feared, that would be hard to take back. Kristine prayed that the three of them would somehow live through it.

Kristine called her mother on the telephone the following day and told her what she had done. Augustina listened in shock. She was hurt and speechless, once again, around a wedding of a dear one – her child – that had taken place without her.

It was a terrible blow to think that her one and only daughter, who meant more than anybody or anything in the world to her, had snuck away and married a bozo who was barely working.

Finally, still in a daze, she exclaimed, "My gosh, you'll have to support him!"

"That's not true!" protested Kristine. "He's going to be working all the time. You'll see!" Staunchly defending him once again, she said that Bill was a very good person! "When you get to know him, you'll see!"

She said Bill was a good person because he was always doing favors for his friends and even strangers without pay! Augustina was not impressed.

Kristine gave up and swallowed hard. She said she wanted to give Augustina her new address and phone number. She had moved into Bill's apartment. His roommate had just moved back East, so it was perfect timing for them. In fact, it was one of the things that made them decide to get married so soon.

"He needed somebody to help him pay the rent!" said Augustina.

"No!" said Kristine angrily. She closed her eyes and took a deep breath as she tried to get a hold of herself so she could talk calmly again. Her voice quivered when she said they wanted to take her out to dinner the following Sunday.

"That's not going to make up for the way you sneaked off and got married!" said Augustina. Her feelings were so hurt that she didn't want to accept the invitation. Besides, Kristine knew her mother didn't like restaurants. She knew that, according to Augustina, home-cooking was the only way to go. But if this was her only chance to get to meet that so-called husband anytime soon, Augustina figured she'd better go. Grumbling, she agreed.

Kristine beamed. "Thanks, Mom," she said. Before they got in another argument, she hurried to end the conversation. "We'll be over Sunday at 5 o'clock to pick you up!" she said. "Good Bye."

Augustina stood there in shock for a little while, then slowly shook her head.

"In *her* car, no doubt," she grumbled under her breath.

On Sunday, all dressed up and ready to go, Augustina nervously waited at her front window.

As Bill and Kristine drove up to Augustina's apartment house, Bill said, "Your mother must be pretty amazing to have such a special daughter like you."

"Well, you have to understand her," said Kristine nervously.

"What do you mean?" asked Bill, surprised.

"Well – you have to meet her," said Kristine. "She's always taken good care of me, but often other people don't understand her."

"I'm sure I'll like her!" said Bill confidently. Kristine wasn't so sure.

When Kristine's shiny blue Studebaker coupe pulled up to the curb in front of her mother's apartment, Bill was driving. Augustina picked up her pocketbook, opened the door and stepped out into the hall. Taking out her key, she locked the door, and walked down the stairs. Kristine and Bill intercepted her in the foyer and greeted her nervously. Augustina was too choked up to greet them with anything more than a clipped "Hello." She shot a curiously hostile glance at the new husband.

When Kristine introduced them, Augustina looked Bill over with suspicion. They didn't touch or try to shake hands. Bill, always smooth as silk when it came time for any type of conversation, was suddenly tongue-tied. It was obvious in a multitude of ways, they did not speak one another's language.

"This is Bill," Kristine said feebly.

"I'm glad to know you," said Bill.

"Yeah," said Augustina, and just stood there looking at him. Dumbfounded, Bill, the actor, the big orator, the proud bodybuilder, was momentarily stunned. Then, with a sweeping, gracious gesture for them to go ahead of him, he managed to say,

"Ladies," and followed them out to the car where he gallantly opened the passenger door and held it open until the ladies were inside and seated across the front bench seat. Kristine stepped in first so she could sit in the middle between her controversial husband and her mother, and make sure her mother didn't burst out with inappropriate comments. Augustina managed to squeeze in beside her, then Bill closed the door. Carrying Kristine's keys in his hand, he quickly made his way around the front of the car and slid into the driver's seat.

"Where's *your* car?" asked Augustina.

"It's at the mechanic's," Kristine said quickly.

"Having the carburetor repaired," said Bill.

Augustina gave him a look that made him very nervous.

"You're not too crowded, are you?" he asked.

"No," said Augustina sharply.

He started the car, shifted the gear, and got ready to enter traffic. Augustina watched the street tensely while Bill waited for a couple of cars to pass. All she could do now was hope he was a good driver. When they finally got going, she determined he was experienced and she relaxed, but just a little.

After the first few blocks of forced small talk, a silence descended on them. Augustina broke it by looking at Bill and asking, "Where do your people live? Kristine never mentioned them."

"Back East in Connecticut," Bill said. "I have two sisters and a brother who's in the Army. I tried to join the Marines but they turned me down because of my flat feet."

Augustina wondered if his feet were as flat as his wallet.

A bright red MG sports car suddenly cut in front of them. Bill slammed on the brakes of the Studebaker as the MG made a hasty right turn and disappeared down the block. Frightened, Augustina said maybe they better quit talking and pay attention to the driving. Bill shut up. Kristine was embarrassed. Augustina's heart was pounding as they drove on in silence.

After about ten more minutes, they reached Hollywood Boulevard and Vine Street where the Pig & Whistle, a popular middle-priced restaurant during World War II, was located.

A long line of eager customers, many of them uniformed servicemen and their dates, waited outside on the sidewalk. The lines were even longer a few years back in the midst of the War, with the large number of servicemen and women passing through Hollywood. On the inside, however, Kristine felt that less emphasis was put on the food than on the exterior that drew people in. But hey, they were in Hollywood and that counted for a lot; they had a marriage to celebrate; and she and her new husband were *determined* to have a great time.

Even though the War was a few years behind them now, crowds were still drawn to the Pig & Whistle on weekends because of its world famous Hollywood and Vine location.

Augustina, her daughter, and new husband waited in line for half an hour. When they finally got inside, they waited another half hour to get a table. People were crowded together jostling one another and having a good time. A hefty young man accidentally stepped on Augustina's little toe that had a painful corn on it. "Ouch!!" she screeched involuntarily. Everyone looked at her and the hefty young man got very red in the face and apologized. Augustina knew he didn't mean to do it, but she wished people could be a little more careful!

When they were seated at their table and her toe had stopped throbbing, Bill took charge and did the ordering. Now Augustina worried about her table manners that were such an issue with Kristine. She didn't want to embarrass herself or have her daughter make snide comments to her later.

Augustina didn't have her reading glasses with her so she had a good excuse for not being able to read the menu. Bill graciously read off the dinner items aloud. Augustina said she didn't want to order anything too expensive.

"Don't worry about it!" said Bill jovially.

With excitement, being the new bride that she was, Kristine started to show off her wedding band, then hesitated for a moment concerned about any negative reaction her mother may have. Augustina reacted with a controlled smile, yet, an uncertain pride welled from deep down inside for her daughter and new husband. Although she was still unsure of the stability of her new son-in-law, she was relieved to have an extended family so close by. With the awkwardness she experienced each time she attempted to make a new friend, Augustina had virtually built no new relationships since the falling out with Art and his family years earlier. So at this point in her life, from her point of view, it was better to have some family, any family, than no family at all. She decided to make the best of this evening of celebration.

Bill and Kristine quietly selected items in the lower price range, offering Augustina a couple of choices.

She wound up choosing fried chicken, then was unable to eat it because she found the pieces too hard to cut and she didn't dare pick them up with her fingers. She resented leaving most of the chicken on her plate. She ate what she could of the rest of the meal - mashed potatoes, mixed vegetables, and a roll and butter - then they all had lemon meringue pie for dessert.

Augustina held her tongue for as long as she could, then criticized the skimpy piece of pie. She said she would rather eat at home. Kristine was embarrassed. Bill laughed and said, "Well, there's no place like home, you know!" But he squirmed uncomfortably. The check came, and it was a big bill to pay in honor of someone who wasn't that thrilled with the meal and this whole damn experience in the first place.

Kristine went to visit her mother a short time after that. They talked and argued about that evening at the Pig 'n' Whistle with Bill. Augustina bawled her daughter out for not bringing him around before they sneaked off and got married at City Hall!

Kristine protested that Augustina had never been friendly to any of her boyfriends in the past, and did not want to risk losing

Bill over her mother's general unacceptance, skepticism, and inability to exhibit couth, particularly for someone as special as Bill. She certainly did not want Bill to be insulted and lose him as she did Arnold from Columbia.

"Well, did he get a job yet?" asked Augustina.

"Oh, that's all you ever want to talk about!" protested Kristine. She sighed deeply. "He worked one day last week on the Alfred Hitchcock TV show. His agent is trying to get him something else. That's the way this business is. No actor works all the time!"

She laughed and said his acting jobs would all come in at once. It seems it's either all or nothing. "I told you, that's just the way this business is!"

Augustina didn't think there was anything funny about sitting around waiting for a job that was so unsure and would probably be a long time coming. She was appalled to learn that he had no sensible trade to back up his acting.

"So he has no bank account and no trade to fall back on. Why couldn't you wait before you rushed out and got married?"

Kristine resolutely insisted that when Bill's career got going, he would make plenty of money.

Their voices rose. They were on the verge of another big argument, so Kristine left.

True to Augustina's fears, Bill was unemployed and home most of the time. His total income was less than Kristine's secretarial job at MGM Studios in Culver City for the past two years. Bill's neglected old car often needed considerable work, so he sold it for a pittance since they now had Kristine's newer Studebaker.

He boasted that each year he collected every dime of the unemployment insurance that was coming to him. He always managed to work enough each quarter to get full compensation the next year when payment was made.

One morning Kristine woke up sick to her stomach and couldn't go to work. By noon, she finally felt better. When the nausea continued every morning for a few days, she and Bill got suspicious. They looked in the telephone book for the name of a doctor not too far away and made an appointment the next day. They said nothing to Augustina about this.

The doctor confirmed their suspicions. Kristine was pregnant. Bill and Kristine pooled their cash on the spot and paid the doctor's modest fee. In a daze they went home.

They didn't have enough money or room in their apartment for a baby. They had hoped to wait awhile before deciding whether or not they were even going to have any children.

Kristine broke the news to Augustina, who became extremely upset. She said it was too soon for anything like this to happen. Thinking about her own struggles raising two children, she feared for her daughter's future. The guilt Kristine felt as a result of her mother's reaction to the situation, along with her own apprehension about her husband's ability to take care of all three of them, began to manifest inside of her. Although she hoped for the best, Kristine knew she had to prepare for the worst.

When severe morning sickness continued and Kristine felt too nauseous to drag herself to work, she quit her job, as did many wives in her predicament. She knew two other women in the office at work and another one of Bill's friend's wife who quit when she was two months pregnant. Bill assured Kristine that he would take care of his family. But when he found out the doctor charged two hundred and fifty dollars to deliver a baby -- the going rate -- he told Kristine he didn't make enough money for them to go to a private doctor. He insisted that she go to the free clinic at the prominent Cedars of Lebanon Hospital in Hollywood. Kristine was very upset. In all the years she grew up with her mother, even through the harshest part of the Depression, neither one of them ever went to a free clinic. The only exception to this was the emergency situation Augustina found herself in when Kristine was five and had that terrible burn accident. During her treatment period, the Kansas City

Children's Hospital didn't ask them to pay for her stay. Although Augustina did not request this generous offer, she always felt guilty for 'taking advantage of the system.'

Finally, Bill convinced her that they had no other choice than to go to a free clinic. With his intermittent acting work over the years, Bill had been a patient there for minor ailments in the past. Kristine, displaying reluctance and a pouting face, went to the clinic, but her confidence in Bill slipped a notch. A young doctor, who had just completed his internship, was assigned to her case. Kristine thought he looked a little bit like Jose Ferrer, a famous Spanish composer and guitarist.

Kristine and Bill went to a Red Cross class on Sunset Blvd. where they learned how to take care of newborn babies. In class, they practiced handling baby dolls as though they were real babies, carrying them and changing their diapers.

They bought Dr. Spock's famous book on child and baby care and read it together on the couch in the evening.

They did not try to talk it over with Augustina or ask her for any advice because they thought she was too old-fashioned to understand the modern way people raised babies in this new era of the 1950's.

On April 20, 1954, Kristine came home from the hospital with a beautiful nine-pound blue-eyed baby boy. They named him Ronny. He was the best-looking baby born in the hospital that day, not red and scrunched-up looking like some of the others, but with the most beautiful fair skin. It was not until later that Kristine and Bill realized that a scrunched up red baby is actually healthy and normal. Soon after birth and while still in the hospital, Ronny became blue. It turned out after three examinations by three different doctors when he was two and a half days old, they were informed that Ronny had an underdeveloped aorta, the main artery of the heart, too small and weak to do the job of circulating his blood properly throughout his small body.

A private pediatrician by the name of Dr. Rupert who donated time to the hospital, was assigned to take care of Ronny's case at no charge. Dr. Rupert was very kind when he talked to Kristine and Bill.

Kristine trusted him immediately. She told Bill she wanted him for their private pediatrician. When Bill said they couldn't afford him, Kristine got mad.

"You may enjoy being a charity case, but *I* don't!"

"But we don't have the money!" said Bill.

"Then *one* of us will have to go to work!" Kristine exploded. She won the battle.

A senior doctor, the head of the Obstetric Ward, overseeing all the patients, insisted that when Kristine returned home she remain in bed for a month. Some conservative doctors still felt that when their patients had Caesarian Sections they should take extra time to stay in bed and heal. With the added concern that Ronny was still blue and it being a touch-and-go situation as to whether or not he would survive, the doctor especially didn't want anything to happen to the mother. So Augustina stepped in and helped take care of the baby for the first month. Though their relationship had been shaky thus far, Bill was glad to have his mother-in-law come to the rescue. Her invaluable help caused Bill to make extra sure Augustina felt as comfortable as possible while she was in their home.

Augustina hopped on the streetcar every day for four weeks to come take care of Kristine and the baby. She constantly worried about where the money would come from to pay their bills, since neither Bill nor Kristine were working. Kristine, like her mother, knew when all was said and done, it would come down to her, not Bill, to take care of the monthly expenses.

After a month, when Augustina no longer came to help on a regular basis, Kristine was stumped as to what to do next.

Although she and Bill considered themselves more modern about babies than Augustina, Bill was too squeamish to change even one damp diaper or take care of the baby's spit-up.

Each time a situation arose in which she needed guidance, Kristine either consulted her Dr. Spock book, called the pediatrician, or got Augustina over there to solve the problem. When she was called upon, Augustina always hurried over and calmly took charge. It suddenly dawned on Kristine that her mother was a much wiser woman than she had ever given her credit for! She now realized what a good mother she was, through thick and thin - through the Depression, divorces, deaths, and becoming a widow – despite any and all hardships, Augustina was her solid rock of Gibraltar. She took exhaustive care of her daughter, always saw to it that food was on the table, even though often it wasn't much, and always went above and beyond to make sure her daughter looked spectacular wherever she went, understanding the importance of first impressions.

In her postpartum state of caring for a sick infant, coupled with her own healing process from her C-Section, it was dawning on Kristine what motherhood was all about. How grateful she was to have a mother who was there for her, who suddenly seemed to know everything there was to know, and who could soothe and appease Ronny when Kristine could no longer keep her eyes open from exhaustion and worry. How her mother's stupid 'Old Country' ways of putting cold washcloths on her baby's forehead to cool his fever, and holding him in the rocking chair bundled in his crocheted sky blue baby blanket with the tiny bears in pajamas on it until he fell peacefully asleep, and standing in the kitchen peeling and chopping as she prepared her homemade soup, were all that mattered to Kristine in during these challenging days.

Bill's father, Frank, who had not been told of the baby's illness, flew out from Connecticut to see his grandson. He was a 78-year-old gentleman who put on an immaculate suit, shirt and tie every day, and walked proudly with his head held high, all of five foot two inches tall. Because there was nowhere for him to sleep in Kristine and Bill's apartment except on the living room couch, he took a room at a modest hotel nearby and stayed there for the two weeks he was in Los Angeles. Although Ronny's skin could sometimes get very blue, most of the time he looked just fine and he smiled a lot, and everyone, including Doctor Rupert, said his heart might strengthen and he might grow out of his condition. Grandfather was very proud of his grandson.

When they were all together, Bill and his father seemed to get along fine. But once when Kristine took the trash out to the incinerator, she heard raised voices and sharp words coming from father and son. Grandfather was berating Bill for not getting a steady job to support his fine wife and son. Bill tried to explain to him about acting, but all Grandfather understood was what he saw. He wanted to help Bill get a job. Bill said he would get his own job. When Kristine came back in the house, not a word was said about the argument.

Kristine generally served meals on one big plate, except for the salad. But when Grandfather was there, it was understood that everything had to be served in a separate dish following his Jewish tradition. It made things a little harder for Kristine. Grandfather's wife, Bill's stepmother, telephoned long distance from Connecticut saying she had been diagnosed with a serious illness and Grandfather had to come home immediately. Although there was some suspicion that his wife was exaggerating just to get him to come home, he decided it was best he go.

Ronny lived for a year and a half. When Augustina heard of his death, she screamed in shock. She was afraid they would blame her, because she had taken care of him so much. Kristine tearfully told her, "Oh, no, no!" assuring her that she knew it was not her fault. The baby was just too little for the operation that would have been the only thing to save him.

The funeral, held at Forest Lawn Cemetery in Burbank, was tragic. Bill cried more than anybody there. Kristine and Augustina comforted one another, too devastated by their grief to speak. Bill's father did not return to L.A. for the funeral. It would have been too much for him to bear.

Three months later, Kristine got pregnant again. In due time, she had a little girl, who was, to their relief, very healthy. A couple of years later, a robust little boy was born, and fourteen months later, they had another girl, also very healthy.

In despair over not getting enough acting work to pay their expenses, Bill had an uplifting bit of luck one day. He ran into Harvey, a fellow actor he knew from the Pasadena Playhouse who had turned to writing when his own acting jobs were too few and far between. He must have been a pretty good writer because Paramount Studios gave him a contract for a thousand dollars a week on the basis of one screenplay he wrote. Currently he was on hiatus – not working in the industry – and being a resilient father of five with a staggering pile of bills to pay, he segued into a lucrative part-time job as a limousine driver working out of the Beverly Hills Hotel, while he waited for his next big writing break.

Bill's ears perked up and when he told his friend about his own circumstances, Harvey whipped out a card from his pocket with the address and phone number of the limo company. He urged Bill to get himself a chauffeur's license and call the company right away to get his name on the list for a driving job. Bill passed his test with no trouble at all.

He loved the job of driving the big luxurious limousines. He loved dressing up in his dark blue suit and looked so confident behind the wheel of the big new Cadillacs and Chryslers. Often, he was able to come home for hours during the day or evening while he waited until he needed to pick up his client to return them home.

He was a conscientious, well-meaning man who would never knowingly hurt anyone or think of letting a bill go unpaid. He borrowed money constantly, mostly from thriving fellow actors he had done favors for in the past and would willingly do favors for again. Since he was bright and loved math and numbers, he helped some friends with their income taxes and got them legitimate refunds they never dreamed they could get.

He took care of writing the checks and handling the finances for their little household, stretching the money to its full limit. His wife trusted Bill implicitly with their family budget, because she herself kept a set of books with a journal for money coming in, and a ledger listing where all the money went out, and their records always matched.

Bill would have made a stellar CPA, but that career path never entered neither his nor Kristine's mind, as his whole world revolved around Hollywood and acting. He did all the shopping and running errands, jauntily driving Kristine's Studebaker around town.

However, Bill made himself ill worrying about providing enough for his wife and children. He hung around the house too much waiting for his agent to call, and took to drinking too much wine that he often bought in gallon jugs, and beer. He took Valium to calm his nerves. He frequently began buying cough medicine because it contained Codeine, which he came to enjoy. Because pharmacists kept records of people who repeatedly bought cough medicine containing Codeine, and would not allow them to buy it after exceeding a certain number of purchases, Bill would go to several different pharmacies around town to get his cough medicine.

When the babies cried and fought the way all siblings do, it upset him inordinately. He thought that family life was supposed to be Paradise from morning till night. Rather than having him upset all the time, to appease Bill when Augustina was not around, Kristine did all the work caring for the children day and night as well as the all the cooking and housework. Both Kristine and Augustina were extremely grateful for the fact that Bill absolutely adored his kids and never complained about carting them around town with him when he ran errands. He relished the moments when people stopped him on the street and in line at the grocery store to praise him for having such beautiful children.

Back at her apartment, in her spare time, Augustina sewed together strips of drapery remnants that she had brought home from the factory in wide strips, making everything from portieres, curtains, jackets, and even skirts for herself.

When the job at the drapery factory came to an end, she decided she didn't want any more sewing jobs, so she found a job taking care of a little four-year-old girl who called her Neeny. Augustina got a kick out of that. She was very comfortable in the job and loved the little girl who always wanted to hold her hand when they walked, but that too came to an end when the child's father got a job back in Chicago and the family moved away.

Bill and Kristine were very sad to receive the news that Bill's father had died. Bill did not go back to Connecticut for the funeral because they had no money for the fare, and just the thought of meeting his judgmental stepmother face-to-face made him break out in a cold sweat. She had been the main reason that Bill came out to Hollywood in the first place when he was eighteen. The two of them could absolutely not see eye-to-eye on any subject. He was not the only one who felt this way. His siblings agreed, and they also left the house as soon as they got old enough.

Bill's father's will was read and they learned that he had left each of his children $2,000, enough for Bill and Kristine to make a down payment on a house. Immensely grateful, they began their search for their new home. They found a large fixer-upper in the San Fernando Valley on a 75 X 150 foot lot. It had a huge fenced yard for the children, a large rose garden with its own fence, a 2-car garage with an attached rumpus room the size of the garage, a vegetable garden in back of the garage, and a separate camellia garden on the other side of the house. The house itself had three bedrooms, a dining room, and one and a half baths.

However, if they bought the house, after making their down payment, they still had to take out a second mortgage. The owner agreed to carry it, but the question was how could they ever pay it back?

When Kristine learned that Augustina was unemployed, she consulted with Bill, then drove out alone to pick up her mother and take her to see the house. Augustina was excited and thought it was marvelous that Bill's father had left him enough money to buy a house.

Augustina fell in love with the rose garden and the camellias, a beautiful crepe myrtle bush beside the clothes line, and the wonderful spacious fenced grounds so the children could safely play. Kristine explained that they needed to take out a second mortgage because the inheritance wasn't enough to purchase the house.

She proposed a plan to her mother. "We figured out we could buy it if I could go back to work for a year and put all my salary toward paying off the second mortgage. But the only way I could do this was if somebody could take care of the children. And I wouldn't want just anybody. Since you're not working now, I wondered if you..." They would turn the dining room into a fourth bedroom and that would be Bill and Kristine's room. Augustina would have the master bedroom so she could have her privacy.

Augustina would not dream of turning them down. Overjoyed, Kristine offered to pay her a little bit each week, but Augustina said she didn't have to.

Augustina was a godsend, for her agreement to this arrangement made possible the purchase of their new home, along with many more opportunities for the children that could not otherwise have been realized.

Augustina was ecstatic to feel appreciated and useful, and wanted the children to call her Neeny, the way the little girl she once took care of did. But she refused to give up her small apartment in Hollywood where she now lived.

Bill thought she should live with them full time, but she disagreed, saying, "You need your privacy and I need to get away by myself on weekends." She would stay five days a week at the house, using the bedroom they provided for her. In the end, this proved to be the smartest decision of all, since it made possible six people living together during the week perfectly viable.

She brought over what she needed during the week in two shopping bags.

Now that she had small children who needed her home in the evenings, Kristine could not work late the way the movie studios often required, especially on short notice when they had to get the scripts ready to shoot, so she got a job as a secretary in a San Fernando Valley aircraft plant a mile and a half from the house.

When Bill wasn't working, which turned out to be most of the time, he drove her to and from work. Otherwise, she took the bus, which fortunately stopped near the plant.

As soon as Bill drove her home on Fridays, Kristine signed her paycheck and handed it over to him. Bill drove straight to the bank and deposited all the money minus pocket money for the week which included buying the kids ice cream on Friday's after school at the nearby Thrifty's. Kristine was indifferent about handling money herself and usually brought her lunch so she didn't have to spend anything on food at work, helping them pay off the mortgage quicker. Because Kristine was so focused on eliminating their second mortgage with her paycheck, Bill had to force her to carry a little cash just in case of an emergency.

On Friday afternoons, Augustina was at the door waiting with her pocketbook over one arm, and a shopping bag in her other hand. As soon as she saw the Studebaker pull up and stop in front of the house, she took off like a shotgun, saying her 'Goodbye' as she hurried down the front walk, beginning her three block hike to the bus stop where she boarded her ride home to her own little apartment in Hollywood for a weekend of blessed privacy.

On weekends, Augustina savored her time to sit quietly, enjoying her potted flowers on the patio, and sometimes to cut out and sew a new skirt or even an outfit for one of her grandchildren. Kristine and Bill heard no more from her until bright and early Monday morning, when she arrived a short time before 8:00a.m., at which time Bill drove Kristine to work.

On a couple of occasions, Bill drove Augustina to her bus stop, but the atmosphere between them had built up over the years to such an intensity due to Bill's lack of a steady job, that they mutually agreed he would no longer give her a ride. As the time went on, and Bill was still not holding a 'decent' job, he was well aware how his mother-in-law resented his lying around the house. Any decent husband should hold down a steady job so his wife (*her* daughter) did not have to leave her children to work all day to bring home a secretary's modest paycheck. From then on, Bill only drove her if it was raining or in other severe weather. Augustina preferred not to be cooped up in the car with him, tempted to say things that would make their relationship even more strained.

In the next two years, Augustina cared for the three energetic, cute, but often tiring youngsters who ran around shouting

'Neeny' whenever they wanted her. She also took pleasure in tending the roses and camellias that grew around their home, watering the lawn, raking leaves, even trimming the tall bushes that grew around the perimeter of the back yard. After the first few months when every spare dollar went toward the mortgage, Kristine was able to adjust her finances and insisted on giving her mother a little spending money since her Social Security income barely covered her rent. When Augustina turned 65, she had refused to take Social Security until Kristine convinced her that it was not Welfare, but a plan that she had paid into while she was working. When Augustina understood this was different from Welfare, over time she looked forward to receiving her minimal Social Security checks to help pay her living expenses. The Oriental lady in the Social Security office gently scolded her for not coming in sooner.

Augustina carried the little ones around when they cried and stretched their little arms up to her. Even the oldest one wanted to be carried when she saw the smaller ones getting so much attention. Often Augustina had to lift them out of harm's way, crying and kicking because they couldn't understand why they couldn't do something that could harm them. Like when the 4 year old boy climbed up on a chair to reach a high cupboard for the small bottle of St. Joseph's Children's Aspirin because it tasted like orange flavored candy, while his little sister eagerly waited below with her hands and fingers outstretched, ready to catch the small plastic bottle. Since Kristine was not fond of sugar in the house, this was no doubt one of the few sweet items the children ever tasted, besides their Friday ice cream treat. In time, this and other normal precarious acts of young, healthy, curious children proved too much for Augustina's small frame. In what spare time she could find, she rubbed liniment on her strained back and rested in a chair with her feet up.

When the last payment was made on their second mortgage, Bill went out and bought a bottle of champagne to celebrate with

Kristine and her mother. For once in a very long time, they all had a happy reason to be in the same room together. Besides the infrequent sit down meal at the kitchen table with the entire family due to random circumstances and an accidental coinciding of schedules, getting together in the same room never happened.

Kristine recognized that her mother was working too hard and she needed a long rest. She decided to quit work and let Bill's limousine jobs and occasional acting work pay their living expenses for the time being while she signed up with a temporary secretarial agency and could work intermittently when necessary.

Half-heartedly, Bill finally admitted that his acting career hadn't paid off. He reluctantly took a full time job as chauffeur to the president of the city's electric company where he worked for several months. But when he overheard his boss and two other electric company officials in the back seat discussing how they thought they could raise the city's electric rates and get away with it, Bill's innate honesty and unwavering integrity superseded his urgent need for a paycheck. He became so angry that he quit his job. Again, he had to make the rounds to his friends, borrowing money to pay the bills. Kristine could no longer take it. Several rifts flared up between them, and along with his love of alcohol sending him into waves of denial of his pressing responsibilities - eventually they separated. Kristine asked Augustina to come back again so she could return to work full time.

This time, Augustina moved into the house without protest. Her "little dab of Social Security" and a little money from Kristine helped her pay for personal things. They argued only occasionally. The things they used to disagree on seemed to pale in comparison to the overwhelming gratitude she now had for her mother. And she knew it was not wise to raise children amid arguments. That was one of the main reasons that prompted her to tell Bill to move out of the house.

Chapter Fourteen

Later, Kristine bought a smaller home in North Hollywood and moved Augustina into a second-story apartment within walking distance, giving them both quiet time away and a break from each other. Kristine believed this was the smart choice to keep their relationship respectful and on good terms. Kristine again paid for Augustina's telephone installation and monthly phone bills, and helped her pay the rent each month. Augustina cursed the fact that there were no sidewalks on her block. On rainy days she had to walk in puddles and gravel and mud if she needed to go to Market Basket, the local grocery store only a block and a half away, if Kristine was not available to go for her, or if she simply didn't want to call Kristine and ask.

As Augustina was settling into her new one bedroom apartment, Kristine focused on furnishing her own home. She bought a new sofa with voluminous cushions. Augustina, who was growing shorter as she got on in years, sank down helplessly into them every time she came to visit.

Kristine also bought a brand-new hide-a-bed, and Sig and Dorothy came out for a week's stay at their house and took the delighted children to Disneyland.

It soon became a tradition, sometimes annually, sometimes biannually, for Sig and Dorothy to drive out from Missouri to visit Augustina, Kristine, and the children. They never had any children of their own, and Kristine's children always jumped up and down with joy when they welcomed Uncle Sig and Aunt Dorothy because they knew it was a sure bet that a trip to Disneyland was imminent.

Augustina was always happy to see Sig and Dorothy, but she declined to go with them to Disneyland. Her decision was a wise one, for it would have proved too tiring for her 70+ year old body to walk all day, and in the event she did accompany them, it was unlikely they could have gotten her to go on any of the rides, especially not the 'E' ticket ones like the Matterhorn Bobsleds!

For the children, the day trip to Disneyland was the most exciting part to their Aunt and Uncle's visit. It consisted of early rising, dressing, eating breakfast and getting inside the big, luxurious, smooth-riding new model Chevrolet. Every two or three years, Sig bought a new Chevrolet. He always kept his cars polished and immaculate.

With no children of their own, Dorothy and Sig escorted their nieces and nephew around Disneyland. Sig wasn't as visibly enthusiastic, though he surely enjoyed himself, but it was Dorothy who demonstrated the most enjoyment. She did not stop smiling and giggling from start to finish, riding the trolley and chuckling in one moment to herself at the surprised look on her little nephew's face when the trolley driver called him by name, reading it off his engraved Mickey Mouse hat.

Upon their return, Augustina had dinner waiting. She happily served her eager, hungry family a hearty German meal of large portions, including generous pieces of homemade apple pie, which Sig always loved. The Boy said in front of Dorothy that his mother was the best cook in the world. Kristine wondered how Dorothy felt about that. Augustina swelled with pride. Her eyes twinkled and she smiled, a little embarrassed. She didn't get too many compliments these days, no matter how much she did for Kristine's family.

Kristine realized how much she always took her mother for granted and seldom told her out loud that she appreciated her. That was just the way it was between her and her mother - a lot of obvious things went unsaid, but deep down, they each knew there was a tremendous amount of love and gratitude they felt for one another.

Before they left to go back to Kansas City, the Boy bought Augustina a 21" portable TV set to use in her own apartment. This became her main connection with the world outside of Kristine's family.

She always watched the News, interpreting it in her own way, which was not necessarily the way it was presented or the way it actually happened. Because of many long, unfamiliar words that were used, along with the fact that her hearing was gradually diminishing, sometimes she told Kristine outrageous stories she thought she heard on the News.

Now that she had her own TV, she picked up free throw-away advertisers from the grocery store or found those left outside on the apartment house lawn, that had the television schedule in it, rather than subscribing to a newspaper which would have cost her 10 cents per copy.

Her small but cozy one bedroom apartment on Vanowen Street was arranged exactly as she wanted it. She still kept a pin cushion with a ribbon attached so she could hang it on a nail in a convenient location in her kitchen, just as she used to do in the old days. During the winter months when her apartment would become drafty, she would spread newspapers on the bathroom floor to help keep the cold from coming up through the linoleum.

She kept half-a-dozen pots of prolific house plants including heart leaf philodendron, pothos, and flowering plants, that flourished inside her home, and she periodically clipped their long strands of deep shiny green leaves as they made their way to the floor and wrapped themselves around furniture legs, then put them in water to start a new plant on another counter or end table. Her watering days were Sundays and Thursdays, religiously.

She still had a large cardboard box of drapery remnants from the factory where she had worked several years before, and occasionally took some out and made something she needed, like an apron with a pocket in the front to place her handkerchief or small scissors, a tablecloth, or an oversized kitchen hand towel.

She had a better, larger mirror in her bathroom to look in now and a full length mirror against the wall in her bedroom, so on the few occasions that she went out, she made sure to check her hair which she always wore in a bun twisted at the back of her head, and her 'chicks' for just the right amount of rouge.

She would look at her reflection in the small wall mirror and say to her daughter, "My hair is getting all gray again. I have to put something on it. Can you come over and do it for me?"

Augustina's hair never turned completely gray. It always had some brown streaks running through it.

She became leery of the telephone Kristine had installed for her.

"They mumble too much!" she complained of the few calls she got. But she always understood Kristine when they spoke on the phone who knew she had to speak loudly and distinctly into the receiver.

"Why did you hang up the phone on me when I called you this morning?" Kristine would ask her.

"I thought you were done talking," said Augustina, who practically never said goodbye on the phone. "Why didn't you speak up if you wanted to keep talking?"

"I did, but you'd already hung up!" With a deep sense of love and compassion, Kristine sincerely wondered if her mother would ever understand fully the ways of modern America.

These days the children were older and Augustina came to Kristine's house just to visit, not to baby-sit or do any housework. It got lonesome up in her little apartment at times and it was good for her to spend time with her family.

Whenever she was asked to stay for a meal, unless it was already cooked, Augustina insisted on cooking it herself. She liked it better that way. Kristine was pleased, too, because after all these years, she found she enjoyed her mother's home cooking more than ever. No matter what she made, it was guaranteed to be delicious.

The children were always put to bed early, by 7:00 p.m., although this was a hard rule to enforce when "all the other kids on the block can stay up later!"

Kristine, who always used to give her mother such a hard time, was now on the receiving end of this seemingly endless conflict between a mother and her growing children.

One Sunday afternoon, Bill came over and took the children to a B'hai picnic in Hollywood. As Kristine was tidying up the house, folding laundry and straightening the living room, Augustina came over and told Kristine she wanted to talk to her. They sat down in the living room, Augustina avoiding the sofa with the huge pillows that enveloped her every time she sat down on it. Augustina said she went to see a lawyer about sending in the card for alien registration that she heard about on television.

"But I *told* you, you're a citizen already! You married an American before 1924."

"Never mind that," said Augustina. "He gave me a card to fill out and send in."

"He said you had to?" asked Kristine, agog.

"Well, I sent it just in case. He said they'd let me know if they need any more information," said Augustina.

Kristine rolled her eyes. "You are *so* stubborn!" she said. Augustina ignored her.

Acquiring and completing her immigration papers was something Augustina kept in the back of her mind ever since she stepped off the ship at Ellis Island in 1908. Although she did not speak regularly about the subject, it bothered her on and off at a subconscious level for the past fifty plus years, and she always wanted to make it right. Being the upstanding woman that she was - full of integrity and never wanting to take advantage of any system or governmental agency - she would never feel settled until she knew for certain that she was a legal citizen of America.

Her lawyer, also knowing by legal standards that she was actually already a legitimately authorized citizen of the U.S., just as her daughter had told her, appeased his client by having her fill out the official paperwork, 'Just in case."

Chapter Fifteen

A few years passed. The children attended the local elementary school, only three blocks from their home. Almost every day after school, when their homework was finished, neighbor children came to play. Sometimes there were as many as ten children romping in and out of the house, shouting and laughing, "taking over the whole damn house," as Augustina put it.

If Augustina was in charge and couldn't even hear the News on the radio because of the children, she snapped at them, "GO PLAY OUTSIDE!!"

"Guy, your grandmother's mean!" complained one of the neighbor children, understandably unable to see it Augustina's way.

A neighboring mother said to Kristine of Augustina's abrupt manner, "I don't understand your mother. I don't understand her at all. But then I guess she's getting on in years."

Kristine laughed, thinking to herself that her mother had been like that her entire life. This behavior couldn't be blamed on old age. That was just her way; she had done so many good things in her life that made up for this one flaw in her personality. It took Kristine her entire adulthood to realize what an incredible mother she had had all these years. Only now could she understand that her mother's sharpness, curtness, and lack of poise and protocol in public situations had simply been the result of a lifelong culmination of witnessing hardships, mistrust, death, and sometimes the too-ugly side of life. Though her heart was huge, no one but Kristine could ever know the kindness and gentleness that lay beneath Augustina's seemingly unpolished surface.

But there was one thing that escaped Kristine. Through her own turmoil, loss, divorce, and daily responsibilities of being a single working mom raising her three kids in the 1960's, it had alluded her that Augustina's strength and pureness was more evident than she realized. It was not only Kristine who saw Augustina's goodness down to the core. It was not only Kristine who saw the kindness and huge-heartedness that knew not how to easily make their way to the surface. Kristine's youngest daughter, though too little to fully comprehend, had been drawn to her seemingly 'crotchety', cranky, grumpy grandma in all her childhood years. Though Augustina did not speak much when she spent time with her grandchildren, and certainly did not hug or kiss the kids, the littlest one always felt an unspoken bond with her grandma.

Augustina called her seven-year-old granddaughter, the same age Augustina was when this story began, to come braid and twist her wispy pony tail up into a bun and secure it with hairpins. "My back hurts today and I can't reach it."

"All right, Neeny," and the little girl eagerly ran to help.

The little girl of seven sat on the sunny back porch with her grandmother in the summer of 1966, combing and braiding her Grandma's waist-length gray-brown hair. She then twisted the braid up into a bun and pinned it to the back of Neeny's head with six or seven hairpins. This special moment was one of her granddaughter's favorite things to do. Spending time with her grandma, sitting together as she combed her hair, was a way to get just a little closer without the awkwardness of her grandmother's still broken, mostly incomprehensible, and unintentionally terse English. It is certain that Augustina, as well, felt the deep bond developing between herself and her granddaughter, though not a word was ever spoken.

Chapter Sixteen

Kristine parked her car alongside the curb in front of Augustina's apartment around 11:00 a.m., as per their arrangements the night before, and went upstairs to get her mother to bring her back to spend Thanksgiving Day with the family. She knocked on the door, and when there was no answer after knocking a few more times, concerned Kristine went to look for the manager, and together they returned with the master key. Knocking one more time with no response, the manager unlocked the door, however was abruptly stopped by the chain attached from the inside. Peering in through the 3" gap, they saw Augustina sitting in her rocking chair, her yellow rotary telephone on her lap with the receiver off the hook. It was determined that Augustina's heart stopped working and her quiet passing from this earth occurred on the eve of Thanksgiving in the year 1968.

AUTHOR'S NOTE

My grandmother, Augustina, died when I was nine years old.

Working on this project for 30 years, my mother and I went through numerous revisions and edits in this story. Regrettably, my mother passed away before it was finished. In her honor, I felt it essential to finish and publish this book.

When I found at the bottom of a storage box in my garage, the Morrison Speller and Workbook – 1930 Edition – with Augustina's vocabulary words and lessons meticulously recorded in pencil in her handwriting, it brought to life her persistence, devotion, and unwavering commitment to learn how to read and write the English language, and become the best mother and U.S. Citizen she knew how to be.

Her Morrison Speller and Workbook – 1930 Edition - also brought this story full circle in representing the timelessness of her circumstances as an immigrant, a single mother, her feeling of never fitting in, and the persistence to keep going no matter what, overcoming the barriers and resistance that permeated Augustina's daily life for 78 years.

Made in the USA
Las Vegas, NV
16 December 2022